W9-BGI-548

# BUDDHIST MEDITATION

# BUDDHIST MEDITATION

**Edward Conze**

Munshiram Manoharlal
Publishers Pvt. Ltd.

ISBN 81-215-0781-2
This edition 1997
First published in 1956 by
George Allen & Unwin Ltd., London



Printed and published by Munshiram Manoharlal Publishers Pvt. Ltd., Post Box 5715, 54 Rani Jhansi Road, New Delhi 110 055.

# GENERAL INTRODUCTION

As a result of two Wars that have devastated the World men and women everywhere feel a twofold need. We need a deeper understanding and appreciation of other peoples and their civilizations, especially their moral and spiritual achievements. And we need a wider vision of the Universe, a clearer insight into the fundamentals of ethics and religion. How ought men to behave? How ought nations? Does God exist? What is His Nature? How is He related to His creation? Especially, how can man approach Him? In other words, there is a general desire to know what the greatest minds, whether of East or West, have thought and said about the Truth of God and of the beings who (as most of them hold) have sprung from Him, live by Him, and return to Him.

It is the object of this Series, which originated among a group of Oxford men and their friends, to place the chief ethical and religious masterpieces of the world, both Christian and non-Christian, within easy reach of the intelligent reader who is not necessarily an expert—the ex-Service man who is interested in the East, the undergraduate, the adult student, the intelligent public generally. The Series will contain books of three kinds: translations, reproductions of ideal and religious art, and background books showing the surroundings in which the literature and art arose and developed. These books overlap each other. Religious art, both in East and West, often illustrates a religious text, and in suitable cases the text and the pictures will be printed together to complete each other. The background books will often consist largely of translations. The volumes will be prepared by scholars of distinction, who will try to make them, not only scholarly, but intelligible and enjoyable. This Introduction represents the views of the General Editors as to the scope of the Series, but not necessarily the views of all contributors to it. The contents of the books will also be very varied—ethical and social, biographical, devotional, philosophic and mystical, whether in poetry, in pictures or in prose. There is a great wealth of material. Confucius lived in a time much like our own, when State was at war with State and the people suffering and disillusioned; and the 'Classics' he preserved or inspired show the social virtues that may unite families, classes and States into one great family, in obedience to the Will of Heaven. Asoka and Akbar (both of them great patrons of art) ruled a vast Empire on the principles of religious faith. There are the moral anecdotes and moral maxims of the Jewish and Muslim writers of the Middle Ages. There are the beautiful tales of courage, love and fidelity in the Indian and Persian epics. Shakespeare's plays show that he thought the true relation between man and man is love. Here and there a volume will illustrate the unethical or less ethical man and difficulties that beset him.

Then there are the devotional and philosophic works. The lives and legends (legends often express religious truth with clarity and beauty) of the Buddha, of the parents of Mary, of Francis of Assisi, and the exquisite sculptures and paintings that illustrate them; Indian and Christian religious music, and the words of prayer and praise which the music intensifies. There are the prophets and apocalyptic writers, Zarathustrian and Hebrew; the Greek philosophers, Christian thinkers—and the Greek, Latin, medieval and modern—whom they so deeply influenced. There is, too, the Hindu, Buddhist and Christian teaching expressed in such great monuments as the Indian temples, Barabudur (the Chartres of Asia) and Ajanta, Chartres itself and the Sistine Chapel.

Finally, there are the mystics of feeling, and the mystical philosophers. In God-loving India the poets, musicians, sculptors and painters inspired by the spiritual worship of Krishna and Rama, as well as the philosophic mystics from the Upanishads onward. The two great Taoists Lao-tze and Chuang-tze and the Sung mystical painters in China, Rumi and other sufis in Islam, Plato and Plotinus, followed by 'Dionysius', Eckhart, St. John of the Cross and (in our view) Dante and other great mystics and mystical painters in many Christian lands.

Mankind is hungry, but the feast is there, though it is locked up and hidden away. It is the aim of this Series to put it within reach, so that, like the heroes of Homer, we may stretch forth our hands to the good cheer laid before us.

No doubt the great religions differ in fundamental respects. But they are not nearly so far from one another as they seem. We think they are further off than they are largely because we so often misunderstand and misrepresent them. Those whose own religion is dogmatic have often been as ready to learn from other teachings as those who are liberals in religion. Above all, there is an enormous amount of common ground in the great religions, concerning, too, the most fundamental matters. There is frequent agreement on the Divine Nature; God is the One, Self-subsisting Reality, knowing Himself, and therefore loving and rejoicing in Himself. Nature and finite spirits are in some way subordinate kinds of Being, or merely appearances of the Divine, the One. The three stages of the way of man's approach or return to God are in essence the same in Christian and non-Christian teaching: an ethical stage, then one of knowledge and love, leading to the mystical union of the soul with God. Each stage will be illustrated in these volumes.

Something of all this may (it is hoped) be learnt from the books and pictures in this Series. Read and pondered with a desire to learn, they will help men and women to find 'fulness of life,' and peoples to live together in greater understanding and harmony. To-day the earth is beautiful, but men are disillusioned and afraid. But there may come a day, perhaps not a distant day, when there will be a renaissance of man's spirit: when men will be innocent and happy amid the beauty of the world, or their eyes will be opened to see that egoism and strife are folly, that the universe is fundamentally spiritual, and that men are the sons of God.

They shall not hurt nor destroy
In all My holy mountain:
For all the earth shall be full of the
knowledge of the Lord
As the waters cover the sea.

THE EDITORS

# CONTENTS

# INTRODUCTION

## *1. The meaning and purpose of Buddhist Meditation*

Meditational practices constitute the very core of the Buddhist approach to life. An intensely practical religion, Buddhism is by contrast inclined to treat doctrinal definitions and historical facts with some degree of unconcern. As prayer in Christianity, so meditation is here the very heartbeat of the religion.

Enlightenment, or the state of Nirvana, is, of course, the ultimate aim of Buddhist meditations. On the way to Nirvana they serve to promote spiritual development, to diminish the impact of suffering, to calm the mind and to reveal the true facts of existence. Increased gentleness and sympathy are among their by-products, together with an opening up to life's message, and a feeling that death has lost its sting. The intended result is stated quite clearly in the verses by which the monks of old testified to their attainment of gnosis (*aññā*). These poems mirror for us the aims of the monks, together with the occasion of the final insight which may spring from any of the meditations outlined in this book. For in them the monks 'tell of the good they have won (*attha*), without bringing in their own ego (*attā*).'[1]

There is, first of all, a deep sense of the perishable nature of all that exists, and a desire not to become again. 'Nowhere is there any permanence in becoming, and there is no eternity about conditioned things. The skandhas rise, and then dissolve again. Now I know that

[1]Anguttara Nikāya iii 359.

this is a reason to feel perturbed. No longer do I seek for further becoming. Freed am I of the objects of sense. All my blemishes are now extinct.' So Uttara's testimony (Th 121–2). Vītasoka, when he had his hair cut, saw that a few had turned grey. This revealed to him the insignificance and triviality of his body,—the darkness vanished from his spirit, and he won through 'to a state from which there is no more coming back to be' (v. 170).

'O would that I who hourly waste, might change
For that which ne'er decays . . .'[1]

In their 'Lion's Roar' these monks often speak of the freedom from anxiety and fear which they have gained. As Sambula-Kaccāna has it, 'So has my nature been transformed by the Dharma that, dwelling alone in this fearful cave, I have no dread, and feel no terror and no consternation' (v. 190). Or, to give as a final example the words of Khitaka (v. 192):

'My heart stands like a rock, and swayeth not,
Void of all lust for things that lust beget,
And all unshaken in a shifting world.
My heart thus trained,—whence shall come ill to me.'[2]

This is the goal of Buddhist meditation as described by the Indian Buddhists themselves.

In other countries things were expressed differently. So we read in Tao-ngan (314–385), a Chinese author, that 'the plane of the practitioner of Yoga is the mysterious hall in which are assembled those who are attuned to the truth. It is the secret chamber of the immortals who prepare themselves to ascend to Heaven. Hard to

[1]Suppiya v. 32.
[2]Trsl. Mrs. Rhys Davids, *Psalms of the Brethren*, 1913. I refer the reader to pp. 420–2 of that work, where 'the aspects of the goal,' as they appear in the *Verses of the Brethren*, are listed, just as those for the Sisters are found in the corresponding volume on pages xxxvii–xxxviii.

climb is this expanse of Non-production, because it is so sublime; hard to cross is this rampart of Non-action, because it is so immense. Through the tiny door, through the mystic opening, the inner court can barely be seen at all. The absolute truth is like the ocean; each day you may bowl out some water, and yet you can never exhaust it. Even so, although countless efforts are made to cause the essence to return to its source, no one can ever fully succeed in doing so. This absolute truth contains the infinite, it is calm, it seems to exist, but cannot be expressed in words. After he has realized it, the saint expounds a teaching without words, he dispenses peace, and reveals insight."[1] This allusive, poetic, and slightly cryptic mode of expression is clearly influenced by Taoism. It is on the basis of his Chinese experience that Reichelt[2] can define meditation as 'a devout reflection about the inmost and highest powers in the universe' (p. 19), as 'the quiet and devout consideration of life's inner meaning, the listening to the voice of Heaven in the soul' (p. 63). Others again define Buddhist meditation as a training which aims at 'satori,'—the intuition of the totality of reality as concentrated in one particular object. Different temperaments and different cultures are indeed bound to react in different ways to the demands of these practices. It would lead us too far here to enumerate all the possible variations, and we now proceed to discuss the central tradition behind them all.

*2. Its range and principal divisions*

Meditations differ according to the objects they consider, or the subjective attitudes they adopt. It is best to say something first about the themes and topics of meditation, and then to go on to the attitudes.

[1]In his Preface to Sangharaksha's *Yogācārabhūmi*, BEFEO XLIV 2, 1954, p. 346.
[2]*Meditation and Piety in the Far East*, 1953.

The Visuddhimagga (iii 105) contains a standard list of 40 'subjects of meditation' (*kammaṭṭhāna*). They are:

*10 Devices:* 1. earth, 2. water, 3. fire, 4. air, 5. blue, 6. yellow, 7. red. 8. white, 9. light, 10. enclosed space: see page 21.

*10 Repulsive Things:* 11. swollen corpse, 12. blueish corpse, 13. festering corpse, 14. fissured corpse, 15. gnawed corpse, 16. scattered corpse, 17. hacked and scattered corpse, 18. bloody corpse, 19. worm-eaten corpse, 20. skeleton: see II 5b.

*10 Recollections:* 21. the Buddha, 22. the Dharma, 23. the Samgha: see I, 1a–c; 24. Morality, 25. Liberality, 26. Devas; 27. Death, see II 4; 28. What belongs to the body: see II 5a; 29. Respiration: see II 1b; 30. Peace: see II 6.

*4 Stations of Brahma:* 31. Friendliness, 32. Compassion, 33. Sympathetic joy, 34. evenmindedness: see III 2.

*4 Formless States:* 35. Station of endless space, 36. station of unlimited consciousness, 37. station of nothing whatsoever, 38. station of neither perception nor non-perception: see III 1b.

*1 Perception:* 39. of the disgusting aspects of food: see II 5b.

*1 Analysis:* 40. into the four elements.[1]

Two only among the forty are always and under all circumstances beneficial,—the development of friendliness (no. 31) and the recollection of death (no. 27). The remainder are suitable only for some people, and under

[1]This considers the body as a compound of the four primary elements, *i.e.,* earth, water, fire and air. It is held to promote the understanding of emptiness, and insight into the absence of a self. I have not included it in my Selections since the views adopted here about physics and physiology differ too much from our own to be even intelligible. In any case, they would carry little conviction, and would have to be re-formulated in terms of modern bio-chemistry.—Other sources (*e.g., Vimuttimagga,* ch. vii, Ehara, p. 121, and Ps, see below, p. 63) give only 38 subjects of meditation, omitting nos. 39 and 40.

quite definite circumstances. The recollection of the Buddha (no. 21), for instance, demands strong faith, and evenmindedness (no. 34) pre-supposes great proficiency in the 'stations of Brahma' which precede it. In this way some of the meditations may be outside a person's range, others may meet with insuperable resistance, others again may fulfil no useful purpose. Because, as such, the exercises have no value in themselves. They are only cultivated as antidotes to specific unwholesome and undesirable states. A Chinese text[1] distinguishes five 'doors of the Dharma,' or five basic themes of meditation:

1. On impurity (nos. 11–20, 28, 39),—to counteract greed.

2. On friendliness (no. 31),—to counteract ill-will.

3. On conditioned co-production (see below),—to counteract stupidity.

4. On breathing (no. 29),—to counteract discursive thinking.

5. Contemplation of the Buddha (no. 21),—to counteract all the four combined.[2]

As a general rule, three kinds of people are distinguished, according to whether they are governed by greed, or by hate, or by delusion. Both the Pali[3] and Chinese[4] sources contain some most interesting essays in characterology, which describe the main attributes and potentialities of the three types. It is, of course, one thing to understand these descriptions, and another to apply

[1]Kumarajiva's *Dhyāna-samādhi* T 614.

[2]Other authorities introduce slight variations into this scheme. T 619 regards the contemplation of causality as an antidote to the attachment to self, and the contemplation of the Buddha serves to overcome the 'submersion of the spirit.' Sangharaksha (ch. 8) has a different fifth item, *i.e.*, the contemplation of the skeleton (no. 20),—to counteract conceit.

[3]VM III 74–104.

[4]Sangharaksha, ch. 6, see 'Buddhist Texts,' no. 198. Kumarajiva's *Dhyāna-samādhi* T 614.

them to oneself and to others. The spiritual discernment of a practised teacher is often a better and more reliable guide.

It would, however, be a mistake to assume that the 40 *kammaṭṭhānas* by themselves exhaust the whole range of Buddhist meditation. They cover only those practices which come under the heading of mindfulness and concentration. In Buddhaghosa's 'Visuddhimagga' they take up 300 pages. Another 250 pages are devoted to meditations which consist in the exercise of wisdom, and which have for their object the skandhas, conditioned coproduction, the four holy truths, and so on. This difference will become clearer as we proceed to the explanation of the basic *attitudes* involved in meditation.

'Meditation' is a European term which covers three different things, always clearly distinguished by the Buddhists themselves, *i.e.*, mindfulness, concentration and wisdom. Their mutual relation is not at once obvious to Westerners unfamiliar with the tradition and terminology. A diagram may help them :

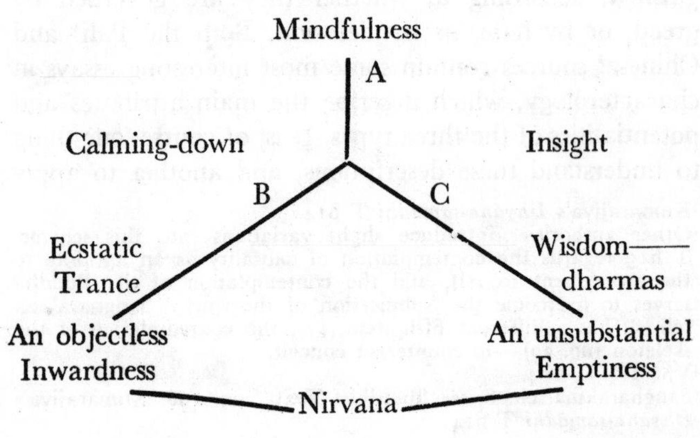

Another bar to understanding lies in the terminology of the traditional presentation of the Buddhist psychology of 'concentration.' It occurs there twice, (1) as a factor essential to all thought, and (2) as a special, and rather rare, virtue.

(1) In its simplest form, concentration is a narrowing of the field of attention in a manner, and for a time determined by the will. The mind is made one-pointed, does not waver, does not scatter itself, and it becomes steady like the flame of a lamp in the absence of wind. Without a certain degree of one-pointedness no mental activity of any kind can take place. Each mental act lasts, strictly speaking, for one moment only, and is at once followed by another. It is concentration which provides some stability in this perpetual flux, by enabling the mind to stand in, or on, the same object, without distraction, for more than one moment. In addition it is a synthesizing activity (*sam-ā-dhi* = syn-thesis), and binds together a number of mental states which arise at the same time, 'as water binds the lather of soap.' Intellectual concentration is found also in unwholesome thoughts. The mind must be undistracted so that the murderer's knife does not miss, so that the theft does not miscarry. A mind of single intent is capable of doing more effectively whatever it does, be it good or bad. The higher degrees of this kind of concentration owe much to the presence of the 'hunting instinct,' and can best be observed in a stoat following a rabbit. Intellectual concentration is a quality which is ethically and spiritually neutral. Many scientific workers have an unusually high capacity for concentrated thought. Not all intellectual achievements are, however, conducive to either peace of mind or spiritual progress. When Sir Isaac Newton boiled his watch, instead of the egg his landlady had given him, he thereby showed the intensity with which

he focused his mind on his intellectual task. But as a result of his intellectual labours a dark shadow has been cast over the spiritual radiance of the universe, and the celestial harmonies have become nearly inaudible ever since.

(2) How then does concentration as a spiritual virtue differ from concentration as a condition of the intellect? Spiritual, or transic, concentration results less from intellectual effort than from a re-birth of the whole personality, including the body, the emotions, and the will. We cannot possibly achieve it without some discipline over the body, since we must be able to endure the prescribed posture, practise the prescribed breathing exercises, and so on. Further, the change of outlook, on which it is built, can well be described as an 'ethical' one. Tradition is quite unambiguous on this point. Before spiritual concentration can be even approached, we must have stilled, or suppressed for the time being, five vices, which are known as the five 'hindrances' (see II 2b), and the observance of the moral rules must in any case have become nearly automatic. Where these hindrances are present, where concentrated thought is fused with greed, the desire to excel, to get a good job, etc., there concentration as a spiritual virtue is not found.

Physical ease, and self-purification, are the first two distinctive necessities of spiritual concentration. The third is the shift in attention from the sensory world to another, subtler realm. The methods by which this shift is effected are traditionally known as the four trances (*dhyāna*), and the four formless attainments. They are essentially, as I have shown elsewhere,[1] a training in increased introversion, achieved by progressively diminishing the impact of external stimuli. It is as a result of

[1]See E. Conze, *Buddhism,* 1951, pp. 100–1. Also *this book,* pp. 113–18.

successful withdrawal and renunciation that the spiritually concentrated release the inward calm which dwells in their hearts. Attention must be withdrawn from sense-data, and everything sensory viewed as equally unimportant. Subjectively, trance is marked by a soft, tranquil passivity, objectively by abstraction into an unearthly world of experience which rises above the world, and bestows a certainty greater than anything the senses may teach. The experience is so satisfying that it burns up the world, and on return to it only its cold ashes are found.

Concentration on an object naturally forms the starting point of the process which leads to the abolition of the object in trance. Buddhaghosa speaks in great detail about the 10 Devices (*kasina*) (see p. 14), which are particularly suitable as initial objects for transic exercises. The 'earth device' is, for instance, a circle of light-brown clay, the 'blue device' a number of blue flowers spread circularly on the surface of a basket, the 'light-device' a circle of light made on the wall or the ground by light shining through a hole, and so on. The disciple must gaze intently at his chosen device, and the effect is probably similar to that of hypnosis, where, entranced by the uniform stimulus of a shining light, or suchlike, we drop objects altogether in the end. As the initial object is subjected to the influence of the transic mentality, it gradually changes its character. At its later stages it is called the 'mental image' (*e.g.*, p. 69), and its transformations have been described with great subtlety.

Finally we must mention that trance admits of degrees of intensity, of course. In the beginning, while the struggle with the hindrances is still unavailing, it is very much like mindfulness. After a time, at the threshold of a fuller collectedness, we reach 'access.' Finally, in 'ecstasy' one-pointedness and abstraction become complete. The elevation of spirit and the transport of the soul then lift the mind above the ken of ordinary men. Some of the exercises lead only to access (*e.g.*, I 1a–c, II 4), others (*e.g.*, II 1b, 5a, III 1b and 2) to full trance.

C. We now come to *wisdom,* the highest virtue of all. To the average person nowadays the word 'wisdom' seems to denote some ill-defined compound made up of such qualities as prudence, a well-developed sense of values, serenity, and sovereignty over the world won by understanding its mode of operation. The Buddhist conception of 'wisdom' is akin to this, but more specific. Buddhaghosa makes its meaning clear when he defines it as that which 'penetrates into dharmas as they are in themselves, and destroys the darkness of delusion, which covers up the own-being of dharmas.'

What then does wisdom meditate about? It may be held to concern itself with three possible topics, 1. true reality, 2. the meaning of life, 3. the conduct of life. Buddhist tradition assumes that the second and third depend on the first. In its essence, wisdom is the strength of mind which permits contact with the true reality, which is also called 'the realm of dharmas.' Delusion, folly, confusion, ignorance and self-deception are its opposites. It is because ignorance, and not sin, is the root evil that wisdom emerges as the highest virtue. A holiness which is devoid of wisdom is not considered impossible, but it cannot be gained by the path of knowledge to which alone these descriptions apply. The paths of faith, of love, of works, etc., each have their own several laws.

As the unfaltering penetration into the true nature of objects, wisdom is the capacity to meditate in certain ways about the dharmic constituents of the universe. The rules of that meditation have been laid down in the scriptures, particularly the Abhidharma. The practice of trance is, as we saw, based on the assumption of a duality in the mind,—between its calm depth and its excited surface. The practice of wisdom, similarly, assumes a duality between the surface and depth of all things. Objects are not what they appear to be. Their true reality, in which they stand out as dharmas, is opposed to their appearance to common sense, and much strength of wisdom is required to go beyond the deceptive appearance and to penetrate to the reality of dharmas themselves.

It is not here my task either to explain the principles of Buddhist ontology, or to give a survey of the countless technicalities of the definition and classification of dharmas. The wisdom which is envisaged in this context as the crowning virtue of the spiritual life is not the wisdom that can be found in the untutored child of nature, the corny sage of the backwoods, or the self-made philosopher of the suburbs. It can operate only after a great deal of traditional information about the Abhidharma has been absorbed. The required skill in metaphysical and psychological analysis would be impossible without a sound knowledge of the material on which this skill is exercised. In some ways this wisdom is analogous to what we call 'philosophy,'—originally, in times long past, understood as the 'love of wisdom.' But just as transic differs from intellectual concentration, so Buddhist wisdom is distinguished from the conceptualized systems of most philosophers by being intent on spiritual salvation, and the extinction of separate individuality.

When do we then know that we have acquired the faculty of wisdom? When a new dimension is added to our view of the world, when we have come to discern the world of *dharmas,* disclosed by wisdom, which is fundamentally different from the world of *things* assumed by common sense. A dharma exists only for one moment, and then disappears, never to return again. But although it vanishes as an existent entity, it can produce an effect long after it has ceased to be. The whole picture is very puzzling to our habits of thoughts, and it requires a special organ, called 'wisdom,' to become visible. Normally we all the time inject personal concepts, and the notions of 'I' and 'mine,' into the presentation of data. To eliminate this habit is not an easy thing to do, and requires great self-denial. 'Dharmas' are objects as they appear to the wise. 'Things' are objects as the ignorant think of them, adding their own connotations and sense of value all the time, without often perceiving that they are doing so. When the ignorant are confronted with this world of dharmas, they are in the position of a dog looking at his master, and trying to puzzle out with his dog philosophy a great deal that is quite beyond his experience.

There can be no wisdom until dharmas have come into view. When they have done so, wisdom admits of degrees, just as concentration does. Traditionally three stages of wisdom are distinguished: learning, reflection, and mental development. Even the relative beginner can greatly increase his wisdom by learning about the basic facts of life, and by discursive meditation on them. On the level of 'mental development' (*bhāvanā*) this meditational technique reaches its maturity, and it then presupposes a proficiency in trance. The previous practice of trance can have taken place either in this, or in a past, life.

### *3. The literary sources*

The *Canonical Scriptures* are replete with references to meditation. The most important single text is the *Sutra on the Applications of Mindfulness* (Satipatthanasutta).[1]

[1]In the Pali Scriptures it is found twice, and also the Sarvastivadin and Mahayana Scriptures contain it.

The bulk of it has been incorporated into this book. It is built up as follows:

I. Mindfulness as to the *body:* (a) Breathing, = II 1b. (b) The four postures, = II 1a. (c) Mindful comprehension of bodily actions, = II 1a. (d) The 32 parts of the body, = II 5a. (e) Attention to the 4 elements. (f) The body in the cemetery, = II 5c.

II. Mindfulness as to *feelings,* = II 2a.

III. Mindfulness as to *thoughts.*

IV. Mindfulness as to *dharmas:* (a) Five Hindrances, = II 2b. (b) Five skandhas. (c) Six sense-fields. (d) Seven limbs of enlightenment. (e) Four Holy Truths, = IV 1.

In the post-canonical literature of the *Theravadins,* three works stand out as special treatises on meditation. The chief textbook is Buddhaghosa's *Path of Purity,* a superb work of 616 pages, written in the 5th century.[1] Like all human authors, Buddhaghosa has his faults. But these are just minor irritants, and he has composed one of the great spiritual classics of mankind. If I had to choose just one book to take with me on a desert island, this would be my choice,—with perhaps a Horace tucked away out of sight in my pocket. The book's appreciation in the West has suffered from the lamentable English translation by Pe Maung Tin, which mirrors its features with the accuracy of a distorting mirror at a fun fair. A better translation has been promised for the Harvard Oriental Series. The second work is Upatissa's *Path to Liberation.* This is a treatise very much on the lines of the Visuddhimagga, but written from the standpoint of the Abhayagiravādin sect, whereas Buddhaghosa follows the Mahāvihāra.[2] Finally we must mention the *Manual of a Mystic,* a Ceylonese handbook of the 16th to 18th

[1] See the Bibliography on p. 179.

[2] The *Vimuttimagga* is extant in a Chinese translation (T 1648). The English translation (519 pages), by the Rev. Ehara, is still in manuscript. We possess, however, a valuable 'comparative study'

century, published in translation in 1916 by the Pali Text Society.

The *Chinese* Canon contains about 20 special treatises on meditation, written or translated between A.D. 200 and 500, and fairly equally divided between Hinayana and Mahayana. Of these works only one, *Sangharaksha's* Yogācārabhūmi (*c.* A.D. 100) is available to European readers, in Professor Demiéville's summary.[1] It is an anthology of extracts from the Sutras, with stories, similes and verses added by the author. Of later works, *The practice of trance for beginners,* by Ch'iang Chih-chi, founder of the T'ien-tai school (522–597)[2] is valuable for its practical hints.

The *European* literature on Buddhist meditation is not very considerable. What there is deals either with the practices of the Southern Theravadin school, of Ceylon, Burma, etc.,[3] or with those found in the Far East.[4] Among the latter, the numerous works of *D. T. Suzuki,* on Zen Buddhism, are in a class by themselves. In 1935 the Buddhist Society in London published a helpful eclectic work, drawing on both Ceylonese and Japanese sources, entitled *Concentration and Meditation.* The book has had a vast sale, and is now in its 10th edition.[5]

by P. V. Bapat, *Vimuttimagga and Visuddhimagga,* Poona, 1937. To it I owe the note on p. 150. The work is older than the Visuddhimagga, in which it is quoted.

[1]BEFEO XLIV 2, 1954.

[2]T 1915. Translated in abstract by S. Beal, *Catena,* 1870, pp. 250–73. In full by Wai-tao and Dwight Goddard in *Buddhist Bible,* 1938, pp. 438–96; also rendered into French by C. Lounsbery in 1944.

[3]F. Heiler, *Die Buddhistische Versenkung,* 2nd ed., 1922; Aelfrida Tillyard, *Spiritual Exercises,* 1927; R. Constant Lounsbery, *Buddhist Meditation in the Southern school,* 1936; reprinted 1950; Nyanaponika, *The heart of Buddhist Meditation,* 1954.

[4]A. Lloyd, *Buddhist Meditations from Japanese Sources,* Tokyo, 1905; K. L. Reichelt, *Meditation and piety in the Far East,* 1953.

[5]At present published by J. M. Watkins (9/6).

### *4. The arrangement of the selections*

The material which this literature places at our disposal is so immense that a book ten times as large as the present one could be easily filled with it. For lack of space, many themes and developments, important and interesting though they are, could not be included. Since a choice had to be made, I decided to concentrate on the main stream of Buddhist tradition. The bulk of the selections are derived from the Old Wisdom School, and in particular from Buddhaghosa's *Path of Purity,* a work of unquestioned authority. No justice could be done to later developments, which often greatly depart from the original impulse. Of the very important Tantra only one extract could be included (III 3). The bhaktic Amida schools, with their visions of Buddhas and their Paradises, are represented by no more than a brief Note (I 4). And the Ch'an school has not been mentioned at all, although it developed a new and fascinating system of meditation, based on koans, and upheld the Buddhist tradition in a typically Buddhist way by denying it.

The order of the selections follows the five cardinal virtues,—faith, vigour, mindfulness, concentration and wisdom. Vigour, however, has no special chapter to itself, because energy is not a separate subject of meditation, but the driving force behind them all.

*Chapter I.* To begin with *faith,* the indispensable starting point of all spiritual life. What is it? Intellectually it is a trusting assent to doctrines not substantiated by immediately available direct factual evidence; volitionally, it implies a resolute and courageous act of the will; emotionally it is an attitude of serenity and lucidity. Buddhist tradition knows three basic objects of faith,—the Buddha, the Dharma, and the Samgha. Two of my selections (I 1a and I 2) deal with the Buddha, who in the first is regarded as the fully Enlightened One, while the second considers his actions as a Bodhisattva, before his enlightenment, as an example which we ought to imitate. The Dharma is here not so much the doctrine of the Enlightened One, as the principle of ultimate reality which is the foundation, as well as the means and the goal of our salvation. The Samgha is not the sum total of all Buddhist believers, nor even the Order of monks. Strictly speaking, it comprises only the saints (*ārya*), in the Hinayana (as on p. 52), the Bodhisattvas in the Mahayana (as on p. 57).

In the recollections of the Three Treasures faith is subordinated to mindfulness, and they may seem rather sober and restrained, without great emotional fervour. This is the way of the Theravadins. The Mahayana has on occasions departed from this restraint, and developed more of what we could call worship and devotion. I had to content myself with one extract here (I 3), but I have appended (as I 4) a Note about an aspect of Buddhism which is not represented in the selections.

II. Next to *mindfulness*. This occupies a central position in Buddhism, much more so than in other religious or philosophical disciplines. 'The Lord has declared mindfulness to be useful everywhere. For what reason? The mind indeed takes refuge in mindfulness, which protects it. Without mindfulness, the mind may not be upheld or checked' (VM iv 49). Or, as we read at the beginning of the Satipatthanasutta, 'the four applications of mindfulness are the one and only way by which beings become pure, which defeats sorrow and lamentation, brings to rest suffering and sadness, allows to enter on the right method, and to realize Nirvana.'

What then is this 'mindfulness'? Like concentration, it provides calm, like wisdom is develops insight,—but both to a lesser degree. It would lead us too far here to survey in detail all the numerous exercises which come under the heading of mindfulness. However diverse, they all aim at guarding the incipient and growing calm in our hearts, that patch of inner calm which may at first not seem very large. A line is, as it were, drawn round this domain, and we keep watch on trespassers at its boundaries (II 5a). In addition, incipient insight is tended and nursed. This concerns very largely the problem of the ego. Distracting forces have the power to act as enemies to our calm when the ego identifies itself with what takes place on the surface of the mind, participating heartily in it. The illusion then arises that these activities are 'my doings,' 'my' concerns, and the sphere in which 'I' live and have 'my' being. Mindfulness begins to dispel these illusions.

In II 1 and 2 we first consider the rather elementary attention given to both body and mind. From his attention to bodily postures (II 1a) the monk derives his distinctive poise. (II 2) A mindful man is further well informed about his own mental condition, and his capacity for introspection is highly developed. His interest in his own mind will not necessarily make him self-centred, as long as he remembers that he has to deal with the rise and fall of impersonal processes. (II 1b) In a class by itself is the attention to breathing. Yogic breathing is of vital importance in bringing about calm. Some of its subsidiary effects, elaborated by Hathayoga, and resulting in bodily relaxation and a great control over the physiological processes of the body, have caught the popular fancy. Buddhist tradition in general has urged restraint in that direction. In the higher and spiritually developed forms of Yoga mental stillness is the aim. And Buddhism goes beyond the pranayama exercises of Yoga in that it treats them as a starting point for meditation on the actual reality of things, by which we assimilate the fundamental truths. I have given here only the initial stages, up to access. The later ones can be found in Buddhaghosa (chapter VIII), Lounsbery, or Sangharaksha (chapter 23).

II 3–5 are then all designed to combat the attachment to the sensory world. They are easy to follow, and little need be said about them. (II 3c) The evils of sense desires are described with great eloquence in many passages of Buddhist literature. The piece selected from the 'Buddhacarita' is more systematic than most. It extends over 46 verses (xi 7–53), and I have been content to give only the similes, which are all taken from the Sutras. (II 4) The meditation on death has been given nearly in full because it is said to be one of those which are beneficial to all and at all times. Buddhists would be inclined to agree with Plato when he says that they are the 'true votaries of knowledge' who 'practise nothing else but how to die or to meet death' (Phaidon 64A). Few things are indeed as salutary as this meditation on death, the inevitable sequel of a life governed by craving and ignorance.

(II 5) The squeamish and the genteel will wish that I had cut down, or altogether omitted, these extracts about the repulsiveness of the body, whether dead or alive. These meditations are, however, of the very essence of the doctrine. This preoccupation with death, decay and filth is often called 'morbid,' and we are told rather to dwell on what is beautiful and creative. It is, of course, true that these meditations are helpful only for some temperaments, whereas to others they are dangerous and harmful. It would also be a mistake to think that they are something that should always be done, all the time and forever. They are part of a greater life, to be balanced with other interests. But it is a fundamental conviction for the majority of Buddhists that the body is an unclean thing, and that it is humiliating to have one. While we love it so much as we normally do, it should be seen for what it is, the passions it engenders must be burned out, the anxieties bound up with it must be overcome by being faced. In a stage of transition these exercises may be useful to get us out of the fool's paradise in which we are wont to live. The beauty of the universe can be seen, without doing harm, only after both dread and attachment are conquered. There is, of course, always the danger of becoming more and more obsessed with one's revulsion, and of adopting a negatively defensive attitude to life. Some of the passages in II 5, as well as in II 3a, may well jar on the modern reader not only because of his own unregenerate condition, but also because they imply some shortcoming in the monkish life. They seem to evince the severe, almost inhuman, asceticism of the Theban desert, and to lack the general sunniness and balance which characterize Buddhist doctrines. They show some of the narrowness and humourless intensity which can be found in eager specialists and absorbed experts all the world over (for instance in the story of Cittagutta on p. 82), and the hoary ascetic can, I am afraid, be rather a bore. But nevertheless this stage perhaps has to precede his transformation into a free and glittering butterfly, and we should not be too hard on him. Allowance must also be made for monkish timidity about sex. It may seem rather absurd to people who have to work with women, and cannot get away from them. If women are habitually avoided, no great objectivity is attained, and one does not feel really safe with them. The art of Ajanta shows that this is not the whole story. But, although the aim should be that one can look women straight into the face, without being touched or affected, some defensive mechanisms are inevitable on the way to that goal.

II 6. Turning away from the senses, the mindful simultaneously turn towards Nirvana. Unthinkable as such and in itself, Nirvana is considered here from the aspect of Peace. It is this which, at a fairly early stage of spiritual development, makes it appear as attractive, an object worth striving for. On the higher plane of wisdom, Nirvana is then compared to the world, and described as a succession of negatives. We are never told what it is, but only how it differs from worldly things. In a manner of speaking it is, of course, something positive, but meditation generally avoids this side of it, as fostering intellectual discussions about something which transcends the intellect, with all its categories and modes of expression.

In the next chapter, on *trance,* I cannot say that I have really adequately dealt with what is a very deep and vast subject, quite remote from the preoccupations of the present day. The first extract (III 1) stresses this very remoteness, without which no further development is possible. But about the psychological mechanism of trance itself, a detailed analysis of the changes which take place step by step in the mind, and concrete advice on how it should be done,—the sources seemed to contain little information. If the subject fails to come to life, it is perhaps because the secret, known 2,000 years ago, has, with so much else, been lost in the meantime. It may also be, because the ancient authorities believed in not being very explicit about mental states which only experience, and no description, can reveal.

In Nagarjuna's great commentary on the Prajñāpāramitā we read that dhyana is the result of three processes, *i.e.* (1) the elimination of desire for the five sense-objects, (2) the removal of the five hindrances, and (3) the emergence of the five factors of dhyana (p. 982).

The first two processes, fairly intelligible in themselves, have been touched upon in II, 3c and II, 2b, and we quite well see that, 'as the sun and moon can no longer shine when hidden by five things,—by smoke, clouds, dust, mist or the hand of Rahu,—so also a man's thought, when covered with the five hindrances, is of no use to himself or to others' (*ibid.*, p. 1020). It is the third point which presents insuperable difficulties, and I have (in III 1b) just compromised with them by a few random extracts from Buddhaghosa.

The next section (III 2), which has our relations to other beings for its topic, is by contrast quite straightforward. In III 3 we then advance to one of those Tantric practices which require previous initiation by a Guru to become effective. The older Buddhism already had regarded psychic powers as one of the by-products of trance, but little importance was attached to them. Transic meditation, breaking through the intellectual crust, opens the mind to the occult cosmic forces, the influx of which leads to supernatural powers. In the Tantra, these forces are personified as deities, of whom there are a great number. This Sadhana on the Goddess Tara has been chosen as the most explicit of all.

Next to *wisdom*. In the order of difficulty the material of wise meditation has been traditionally arranged under the five skandhas, the 12 links of conditioned co-production, and the four holy truths. Numerous meditations have first of all been devised to bring about a thorough familiarity with the five skandhas. The disciple must learn to recognize them everywhere. By way of example I give the situation by which Sangharaksha (chapter 4) illustrates the simultaneous functioning of the five skandhas with regard to one single object: If a man finds a necklace in the street, then the sight of it is 'form,' his pleasure in finding it is 'feeling,' the operation by which he recognizes it as a 'necklace' is 'perception,' the desire to take it is 'impulse,' and the discriminative awareness of it 'consciousness.' Much is then to be done regarding the distinctive properties of the five skandhas, their subdivisions, mutual relations, and all the time the absence of a self, person, etc., in them must be kept in mind. The consideration of the five skandhas then leads easily to the links and the truths. 'When he considers what the cause of these skandhas is, he sees that they are caused by ignorance' (Ps. x 112). Less obviously, the mindful awareness of feeling is identical with the truth of ill (Ps. x 119), and so on.

In this book a different arrangement has been adopted. Without the vivifying influence of a living teacher the meditations on the skandhas look rather dry and dusty, and make bad reading. So we begin, IV 1, first with the holy truths, in which the Buddha first announced, in the Sermon of Benares, his discoveries about the nature of reality. IV 1a. The traditional formula easily lends itself to expansion into a series of meditations. We give here the gist of what Buddhaghosa has to say about the first truth of ill. For the other three the reader must be referred to the Visuddhimagga (xvi 61–83).

IV 1b. The sixteen aspects of the four truths, greatly prized in later tradition, have been included as an example of a rather advanced form of meditation, fit only for saints. The four truths are by no means the ABC of Buddhism, to be grasped immediately by the average educated person, as some European books seem to suggest. Originally they were *statements* about the nature of the world and the deliverance from it. In the course of time they were interpreted as the four basic *facts* of life, *i.e.,* the fact that there is ill, that it originates, that it stops, that there is a path which leads to its stopping. Each of these four facts was further considered from four different angles. The resulting list of 16 items must have developed after the division into separate schools (*c.* 200 B.C.), for the lists of Theravadins (VM xxii 97–103) and Sarvastivadins do not agree. In this case I give the Sarvastivadin account, not because I regard it as older or more authoritative, but because the Sarvastivadin documents are here the more explicit of the two.

Fundamental to all the meditations which are guided by wisdom is the antithesis between conditioned and unconditioned dharmas. The first step is to get the conditions into view and to survey them (IV 2–3), the next to withdraw from conditioned things as such (IV 4), and the last to turn to the Unconditioned, the emptiness or Nirvana. As to the first, I have given the description of some of the more elementary exercises, followed by a summary (IV 3c) of the 12 links of the chain of causation. The formula of conditioned co-production, deep and not easy to grasp, offers an explanation of the fact that we are 'spirits ill at ease,' under the sway of karma, suffering and worldly conditions. It is not likely to interest those who either do not know that they are under karma, or who treat this, not as a cause for wonder, but as a natural fact. The Buddhists have considered this formula as the supreme insight of a Buddha, it was with them a subject of constant meditation, and in addition the presence, in the vestibule of monasteries, of the famous 'wheel of life' (*saṃsāra-maṇḍala*) served as a constant reminder of its crucial importance. Although 'this law is deep, and also looks deep,' nevertheless Buddhaghosa's account, summarized here, appears quite coherent, and presents no insuperable difficulties.

(IV 4) The description of the eight stages, by which the disciple proceeds to the rejection of all conditioned things in favour of the Unconditioned, has always struck me as exceptionally masterly and powerful, bearing the stamp of truth on every word of it. These meditations lead directly to the spiritual rebirth of sainthood, and are followed by two further stages which I have omitted (*i.e.,* 'Adaptation,' xxi 128, and 'Adoption' and 'Path Knowledge,' xxii). (IV 5) After the rejection of all conditioned things, 'Emptiness' becomes the 'proper pasture of holy men.' It may surprise the worldling to learn that an inexhaustible variety of interest lurks in this subject of emptiness. No justice can be done to it here. In the *Mahabodhi Journal* (63, 1955, pp. 203–11) I have described 33 different kinds of 'emptiness.' The one extract which I can give here will, I hope, stimulate the reader to further research into this fascinating field of enquiry.

A few remarks about the *principles of my translation* may not be out of place here. I have aimed at being as literal as I could be, without becoming positively unintelligible or repulsively clumsy. The result is not always idiomatic English. As a matter of fact, the text reads like a translation. That is nothing really to wonder at, because in fact it *is* one. Works on meditation are technical treatises, written not for pleasure but for instruction. The translator's chief task is the scrupulous transmission of their contents. Often he has no choice but to closely follow their syntax. The Buddhist translators of the past, in China, Tibet and Japan, have evolved a style of their own, much at variance with the language of secular works. Now that the scriptures are being translated into a new world language, I see no reason to depart from the conventions of my predecessors. The 'awkward earnestness,' with which Buddhist translators have been charged may be less due to their lack of literary skill, than to an overriding desire for fidelity.

In the interest of greater readability I have, however,

often abbreviated Buddhaghosa, and eliminated laboured etymologies, verbal repetitions, irrelevancies and redundancies. Some passages, rather too diffuse for modern taste, have been summarized. Many minor stylistic adjustments have been made, without, however, touching the sense of the original. And verse has been rendered as prose where the Pali is mere doggerel (as on pp. 122, 141–2).

Every technical subject has its own terminology, and Buddhaghosa wrote for people who knew theirs. In order to derive benefit from these selections, the reader ought to be already fairly well informed about the meaning of such terms as 'conditioned co-production,' the 'four applications of mindfulness,' 'supramundane,' and so on. All these elementary things have been carefully explained in my *Buddhism* book, and in the glossary to *Buddhist Texts through the Ages*. There is no point in going all over them again, because otherwise we would never come to the main theme of the book at all. Some subjects evaporate when treated in the language of the nursery. Even so there remains a residue of difficult terms and phrases. Particularly puzzling are some of the ideas taken for granted here on such subjects as medicine and the natural sciences. To give just one instance, the 'worms' on p. 89 are not easily identified in terms of the current lore about the subhuman inhabitants of our bodies. Are they viruses, or germs, or are they some mythological vermin? If every difficulty had been explained, the book would have had to be burdened with extensive notes. The main outlines of the argument are perfectly clear, and some of the details have just to look after themselves.

### 5. *Buddhist Meditation and Modern Psychotherapy*

Mental health is the goal both of the practitioner of meditation and of the modern psychologist. Apart from that there is little contact or similarity between them. They differ profoundly in their definitions of mental health, in their theoretical assumptions about the structure of the mind and the purpose of human existence, and in the methods which they prescribe for the attainment of mental health. In recent years a few psychologists have shown some interest in the therapeutical value of these meditations.[1] Little has come of it, and this is not surprising in view of the resistance which these meditations are bound to encounter. It is agreed that anxiety is an undesirable state which ought to be removed,—but what would modern psychologists think of Sangharaksha's (chapter 7) specifics for the removal of fear? Sangharaksha claims that anxiety will be dispelled if we think of the excellence of the merits of the Tathagata, or his image, of the Dharma, of the Samgha, or if we meditate on morality and its prohibitions, if we comprehend emptiness, study the six elements and twelve links, or practise compassion. A modern psychologist will not be able to claim that these measures are incapable of removing anxiety, but he will rightly maintain that they are not likely to have much effect on his patients as he finds them.

Contemporary psychology is a product of modern civilization. Its main aim is to help the mentally disturbed to greater adaptation to the conditions of our

[1]The pioneer work of Geraldine Coster, *Yoga and Western Psychology,* 1934, throws light on the Yoga practices of Patañjali, from the point of view of orthodox Freudian psychoanalysis. A number of Svamis, like Akhilananda (*Hindu Psychology,* 1947) have written on the subject, usually to the detriment of European psychology. In numerous prefaces and one separate article 'On the Psychology of Eastern Meditation' (in *Art and Thought,* 1947, pp. 169–79) Jung has explained his views, which owe so much to the inspiration of Chinese and Gnostic traditions. There is also a recent article by A. W. Watts on 'Asian Psychology and modern Psychology' in *American Journal of Psychoanalysis,* xiii, no. 1, 1953.

society, to keep them going within it. The meditations outlined here, on the other hand, are meant for people who do not only not want to adapt themselves to modern civilization, a phenomenon unknown to them, but also to any form of social life, and who want to get out of the world altogether. The upper ranges of the virtues of mindfulness, concentration and wisdom demand a reformation of the conduct of life which is greater than almost any layman is willing to undertake. The higher mindfulness, and nearly the whole range of concentration and wisdom, presuppose a degree of withdrawal from the world which is incompatible with the life of an ordinary citizen. Those who are unwilling to make the sacrifices necessary to achieve a radical seclusion from the world can practise these virtues only in a very rudimentary form. It is quite idle to pretend that they do not involve a complete break with the established habits of life and thought.

The meditations can further thrive only in the climate of a living spiritual tradition, which to some extent guarantees their basic assumptions and success. Modern psychology operates in circles whose members are strangers to the spiritual tradition of mankind. They can easily grasp the impact of physical, chemical and social, as distinct from spiritual, forces. Electric shocks, injections, or the manipulation of childhood experiences do not presuppose any acquaintance with the spiritual realm. Even the Jungian system, so friendly to religion, bears signs of having been nurtured in an environment of unbelievers. While trying to take note of the spiritual tradition of mankind, it pays undue attention to the more phantastic and debased aspects of its magical and psychic side, and true spirituality is treated as irrelevant. Compared with modern psychology, the Buddhist meditational practices suffer at present from at least four disabilities, which stem from the mentality of the average Westerner, and the conditions he has created around him:

1. Modern individualism, the pretences of democracy, and the current methods of education have combined to produce a deeprooted dislike for mental discipline. This shows itself, first of all, in an aversion to memorizing the salient points of various meditations, not to mention the numerical lists (see pp. 174–6), which are the very backbone of the entire training. Many of our contemporaries fall by the wayside already at the initial and quite elementary, though indispensable, point of memory training. How can these points be meditated on unless they are first retained in the memory? Secondly, in addition to learning the texts by heart, we are also expected to accept them literally as they stand. This runs counter to the habit of indefinitely arguing about everything, and to the ideal of 'using one's own judgment.' Finally, our contemporary feels quite at home when called upon to 'express his personality.' Here, however, he is asked to train it, to drill, and ultimately suppress it. A friend of mine complained rather drastically that the Buddhists seemed to treat their minds like an assembly of performing fleas. That is, indeed, what they are doing.

2. Only a few of the more elementary exercises can be carried out in conjunction with other duties. The remainder is reserved for professionals, and requires the total retirement of a monastic life, in which they can be pursued regularly and without intermission. The destruction of the monastic life was the first prerequisite of industrial civilization, which has now succeeded in closing nearly all the avenues of escape. Even a temporary retreat is no longer easy to come by.

3. A third point, though it may seem trivial, is quite decisive. The level of noise is at present everywhere far too high. No one can get away from cars, motor cycles, wirelesses, and from aeroplanes which pursue us even into the quiet of the countryside. 'Noise is a thorn in the side of dhyana,' as the ancients have told us. Its ubiquitous and distracting effects give additional force to Peguy's definition of modern civilization as 'one vast conspiracy against the spiritual life.'

4. No textbook can give more than shorthand notes in fairly general terms. The concrete application of the instructions is greatly helped by the advice of a spiritual guide, who is also in a position to decide which practices are suitable in particular individual circumstances, and which ones are not. Clearly I cannot be expected to act as a Guru in print. As for living teachers, there is a great dearth of them. We must usually console ourselves with the old saying that 'when the time is ripe, the Guru appears.'

For these, and other, reasons the methods of Buddhist meditation are nowadays less likely to be fruitful than they were in days past. The elaboration of other methods for the improvement of mental health must therefore be welcomed. It would, however, be a mistake to assume that the modern world is having it all its own way. Discontent with modern life is widespread, and a great spiritual hunger makes itself felt in all classes of society. One cannot pretend that a little book like this one contains all the information necessary for salvation. Within its limitations it may, however, give some guidance to the children of the light who are still dispersed in our midst. And even the others may find in it some historical and psychological information, as well as plenty of food for discussion.

# SELECTIONS

# I

## DEVOTIONAL EXERCISES

### I. THE THREE TREASURES

#### *a. The Recollection of the Buddha*

(*The formula*): The Yogin who is endowed with trusting faith, and who wants to develop the recollection of the Buddha should, in a suitable dwelling place, in solitude and seclusion, recall the virtues of the Buddha, the Lord, as follows: *'This Lord is truly the Arahat, fully enlightened, perfect in his knowledge and conduct, well-gone, world-knower, supreme, leader of men to be tamed, teacher of gods and men, the Buddha, the Lord.'*

(*The 10 points of the formula*): 1. (a) Because he is at a great distance (*āra-ka*) from the defilements, stands quite far away from them, has, by means of the path, destroyed the defilements together with their residues,—therefore he is an *Arahat,* on account of this distance. (b) And since by that path he has slain (*hata*) the foes (*ari*) *i.e.,* the defilements, he is an Arahat on account of his having slain the foes. (c) And since the Lord knows conditioned co-production in all respects, he cognizes its constituents as they really are, turns away from them, detaches and frees himself from them, and he has broken (*hata*), destroyed and demolished the spokes (*ara*) of this wheel of Samsara. In this sense also is he called an Ara-hat. (d) And he is an Arahat because he is worthy (*arahati*) of the highest gifts; for he is worthy to receive the robe and the other requisites, as well as special worship. (e) And finally he is unlike certain fools in this world who imagine that they are wise, and who, afraid of a bad reputation, do evil in secret; therefore he is also an Arahat on account of the absence of secret (*raha*) evil-doing.

2. He is the *Fully Enlightened* (*sammāsaṃbuddho*) because he has understood (*buddhattā*) all dharmas correctly (*sammā*) and by himself (*sāmam*).

> 'What should be known, that I have known;
> What should developed be, I have developed;
> What should forsaken be, that I forsook.
> Hence, Brahmin, am I Buddha,—One Awake'
> (Sn 558).

3. He is *perfect in his knowledge and conduct:* Here 'knowledge' refers to either the three, or the eight, kinds of knowledge. 'Conduct' comprises these 15 dharmas: (1) moral restraint, (2) guarding the doors of the senses, (3) moderation in eating, (4) cultivation of vigilance, (5)–(11) the seven good dharmas, and (12)–(15) the four formless trances. These 15 dharmas are called 'conduct,' because by them the holy disciple conducts himself, or moves in the direction of the Deathless. And here the perfection of the Lord's knowledge brings about his omniscience, and his perfection of conduct his great compassion. Through his omniscience he has understood what is, and what is not, salutary to all beings: with his great compassion he wards off that which is not salutary, and joins them to what is salutary. Just so someone perfect in knowledge and conduct would act.

4 (a). 'Gone' (*gata*) can refer to his 'journey' (*gamana*), which, in the case of the Lord, is auspicious, quite pure and faultless. And what is that journey? The holy path. By that journey he has gone without hesitation to the place of Safety,—therefore, from his auspicious journey

he is called the *'Well-Gone.'* (b) Or he has gone to the exquisite place, the deathless Nirvana; he then is 'Well-Gone' in the sense that he has gone to the place where all is well. (c) Or he has gone rightly, without again going back to the defilements which he has forsaken on this or that path (*i.e.,* that of a Stream-winner, etc.). Or he has 'gone rightly,' from the time that he fell at the feet of Dipankara to the time when he sat on the terrace of enlightenment; during all that time he has worked for the weal and happiness of the entire world by his right progress, which consisted in the fulfilment of the thirty perfections; and he kept out of the way of the extremes, rejecting the doctrine of eternity as well as that of annihilation, and avoiding both sense-pleasures and self-torment.

5. He is the *world-knower,* because he has known the world in all respects. For the Lord has known, understood, and penetrated the world in every way,—its own-being, its origination, its cessation, and the expedient which leads to its cessation.

6. He is *supreme,* because no one is superior to him, or more distinguished in virtues than he is.

7. *Leader of men to be tamed:* He leads men who can be tamed. He 'tames' means that he disciplines them.

8. *Teacher of Gods and men:* He instructs others, each one according to his worth, in the ultimate truths regarding this life and the next one.

9 (a). He is the *Buddha* because, whatever there may be that is cognizable, all that he has known (*buddhattā*) through the cognition which constitutes his final deliverance. (b) Or, because he himself has understood (*bujjhi*) the four Truths, and caused other beings to understand (*bodhesi*) them.

10. *Lord* (*Bhagavat*), finally, is a term which denotes respect and reverence for him who, through the dis-

tinction of his virtues, is the highest among all beings.

(*The results*): The heart of him who recalls the virtues of the Buddha, by way of recollecting that for such and such reasons the Lord is an Arahat, Fully Enlightened, and so on, 'is not obsessed by greed, hatred or delusion, and his mind becomes quite straight with reference to the Tathagata' (A iii 285). When, in the absence of obsession with greed, etc., the hindrances are impeded, and the mind has become straight by facing towards the subject of meditation, then (1) applied and (2) discursive thinking can turn towards the Buddha's virtues. Thinking is repeatedly applied to them, the practitioner discourses to himself about them, and as a result (3) rapturous zest arises in him. After he has felt rapturous zest, (4) the tranquillity which is based on it makes the cares of body and mind subside. When his cares subside, (5) a feeling of happiness, both mental and physical, arises in him. Happy, with the virtues of the Buddha for his object, he concentrates his mind. In this way the (five) Jhana-limbs arise in due order in one single moment. But because of the profundity of the Buddha's virtues, and the effort required to keep in mind virtues of so great a variety and manifoldness, the trance does not reach full ecstasy, but only access.

And the monk who is devoted to this recollection of the Buddha is respectful and reverent to the Teacher; reaches an abundance of faith, mindfulness, wisdom and merit; is always full of zest and joy,; overcomes fear and dread; is able to bear pain; obtains a sense of intimacy with the Teacher; and his body which has embodied this recollection of the Buddha is, like a shrine, worthy of worship; his mind steers in the direction of Buddhahood; when he is confronted with reprehensible situations, a sense of shame and a dread of blame are set up in him, as though he saw the Teacher before him. Even if he does not penetrate any further, he is at least bound for a happy rebirth.

### *b. The Recollection of the Dharma*

(*The formula*): If he wants in addition to develop the recollection of the Dharma, he should, in solitude and seclusion, recall its virtues as follows: '*Well taught has the Lord the Dharma, it is verifiable, not a matter of time, inviting all to come and see, leading to Nirvana, to be known by the wise, each one for himself.*' This (formula) refers partly to the Dharma in the sense of Scripture, and partly to the ninefold supramundane Dharma (comprising the 4 paths, the 4 fruits, and Nirvana). For the term 'well-taught' refers also to the Dharma in the sense of Scripture, but the other expressions only to the supramundane Dharma.

(*The 6 points of the formula*): 1. The Dharma, in the sense of Scripture, is *well taught* because (a) it is lovely in the beginning, middle and end, and (b) because, true in its meaning, and true in the letter, it reveals the holy life completely fulfilled and in its entirety. (c) Or, it is 'well taught' because it is essentially free from perversion. The teachings of non-Buddhists are essentially subject to perversion: dharmas they describe as obstacles actually are no obstacles, and those they describe as conducive to salvation actually are not conducive to salvation: hence these dharmas are badly taught. The essential substance of the Lord's Dharma is not similarly subject to perversion, because when some dharmas are called obstacles, and others conducive to salvation, there is in actual fact no transgression of the actuality of the dharmas so described.

(d) The supramundane Dharma, moreover, is well taught, because it consists in the annunciation of a progressive path which conforms to Nirvana, and of a Nirvana which conforms to the progressive path. As it has been said : 'Well has the Lord pointed out to his Disciples the progressive path which leads to Nirvana. For Nirvana and the Path flow together, just as the waters of the Ganges flow together with those of the Jumna, and unite with them' (D ii 223).

2. *Verifiable*—(a) as to the holy path, it can be seen by the holy disciple himself as soon as he has effected in his own continuity the absence of greed, etc. (b) Or, as to the ninefold supramundane Dharma,—one who has attained it, he himself can see it by means of a cognitive and reflective contemplation, and does not need to go by a belief in others.

3. *Not a matter of time,*—it does not take any time to yield its fruit. It is so called because it does not yield its fruit after say five or seven days have passed, but immediately after it has manifested itself.

4. *Inviting all to come and see,*—because it is capable of inviting to 'come and see this Dharma !' And how is it capable of doing so ? Because it actually exists, and because it is perfectly pure. This ninefold supramundane Dharma actually exists in its own-being, and it is perfectly pure like the full moon in a cloudless sky, or like a genuine precious stone placed on a pale woollen cloth.

5. *Leading to Nirvana,*—the holy Path leads to Nirvana. In its turn the Dharma which consists of Nirvana as the fruit is fit to lead up to that which should be realized.

6. *To be known by the wise, each one for himself,*—all the wise, *i.e.*, those of great intellectual capacity, and so on, should understand, each one for himself, that 'I have developed the Path, attained the fruit, realized ces-

sation.' For it is not through the master's developing of the Path that the pupil's defilements are forsaken; nor does he live in peace because the master has achieved the fruit; nor does he realize Nirvana because the master has done so. Therefore one should not look upon this Dharma as if it were a diadem on someone else's head. But it is precisely in his own mind, so it is said, that the wise must see and experience it. And this lies beyond the reach of fools.

### *c. The Recollection of the Samgha*

If he wants to develop the recollection of the Samgha, he should, in solitude and seclusion, recall the virtues of the Samgha as follows: '(*I*) *Well-behaved is the Community of the Lord's disciples, straight is their behaviour, proper and correct.* (*II*) *The four pairs of men, the eight persons,—these are the Community of the Lord's disciples.* (*III*) *Worthy they are of offerings, worthy of hospitality, worthy of gifts, worthy of respectful salutation, they, the world's peerless field of merit.*'

I. Here *well-behaved* means that they (the saints) are on the right path of progress, the path which does not lead backwards but forwards, which presents nothing hostile, and which conforms to the Dharma. . . . And because this path of right progress is *straight,* not crooked, not curved, not bent, because it is also called the noble '*proper* norm,' and as befitting is considered as *correct,* therefore one also says that the holy Samgha (of the saints) who behave in such a way is 'straight in behaviour, proper and correct.'

Moreover, they are (Ia) *well-behaved* because they progress in the well-taught Dharma-Vinaya according to the instructions given therein, and because they progress on a path which is the only sure one. (Ib) Their behaviour is *straight* because, avoiding the two extremes, they progress on the middle way, and because they strive to forsake faults in acts of body, speech and mind that are crooked, curved and bent. (Ic) Nirvana being the proper norm, the Samgha's behaviour is *proper* because the saints progress towards that as their goal. (Id) They are *correct* (*sāmīci*) because they progress in such a way that they become worthy of the services which juniors render to seniors.

II. *The four pairs of men:* there are four pairs of men in the sense that those established in the first Path and in the first Fruit count as one pair, and so for the other three Paths. *The eight persons,*—when they are considered as individuals, there is one on the first Path and one at the first Fruit, and so we get eight. A 'person' here means 'one who can be disciplined.' . . .

III. *The world's peerless field of merit,*—a quite incomparable piece of ground on which the merit of all the world can grow. Just as the piece of ground where a king's or minister's rice or barley are growing is called the king's rice-field or the king's barley-field, just so the Samgha is the piece of ground on which the merits of all the world can grow. For it is thanks to the Samgha that there is the growth of the merits of the world which are conducive to so manifold and so various benefits and happiness.

### 2. THE BODHISATTVA'S EXAMPLE

(When he is bothered by anger or hatred, the disciple) should contemplate the virtues of the Teacher's former conduct. And this is the manner in which he should contemplate it: Listen, you recluse, is it not a fact that your Teacher, before his full enlightenment, when he was still a Buddha-to-be (*Bodhisatta*) who had not yet won full enlightenment, while he was, during four incalculable periods and one hundred thousand (smaller) periods fulfilling the Perfections, on many occasions showed no anger for his enemies, even though they were intent on killing him? For instance:

(a) In the birth story of Sīlavā he did not allow his ministers even to touch a weapon, when they arose to ward off the rival king who had seized a large portion of the kingdom, having been brought in by a bad minister who had misconducted himself with his own queen. And further on, when he was buried up to the neck, together with a thousand of his followers in a charnelfield, he felt not even the slightest anger in his mind. When the jackals came along to devour the dead bodies, he exerted his manly strength to remove the earth, and thus saved his life. With the help of a Yaksha he then climbed into his own bedroom, and when he saw his enemy lying on the royal bed, he did not become furious, but placed him into the position of a friend, and made a sworn pact with him.

(b) In the birth story of Khāntivādi the wandering ascetic was asked by the foolish king of Kāsi what doctrine he preached. When he replied, 'I am a teacher of forbearance,' he was cruelly flogged with spiked whips and his hands and feet were cut off. And yet he did not show the slightest anger.

(c) It is perhaps not so wonderful that an aged monk should behave in such a way. But in the birth story of Cūla-Dhammapāla the same is reported of an infant. 'Dhammapāla's arms, perfumed with sandalwood oil, are being cut off, though he is heir to the kingdom. My breath, O king, is about to cease!' So lamented his mother, when his father, king Mahāpatāpa, had both his hands and feet lopped off, as if they were bamboo-shoots. Not content with that, he also ordered his head to be cut off. Dhammapāla then said to himself: 'Now is the time to restrain thy heart. May thy heart become evenminded towards these four,—the father who has ordered my decapitation, the men who will carry it out, my weeping mother and myself.' Firmly abiding in his undertaking, Dhammapāla did not show the slightest trace of anger.

(d) It is perhaps not so wonderful that as a human being he should behave in such a way. But even as an animal, when he was the elephant Chaddanta, his mind felt no anger for the hunter who brought him misfortune when he pierced his navel with a poisoned arrow. As it has been said: 'Afflicted with a huge arrow the elephant addressed, without anger in his mind, the hunter, and said: For what object, for what reason, my dear friend, do you kill me? And who was it that instigated you?' When the hunter replied that he had been sent by the queen of Kāsi for his tusks, Chaddanta, in order to meet her wishes, broke off his own tusks, which were beautiful and lovely, resplendent with the emanation of rays in the six colours, and gave them away.

(e) When he was the king of the monkeys, he had saved with his own hands a man from falling down a precipice in the mountains. But the man thought to himself: 'Monkeys are the food of men, just like the other wild beasts of the woods. In my hunger I will therefore kill and eat this monkey. Well fed I will then go my way, a great deal of meat I will take with me, and so I will get out of this wilderness and have some provisions for the way.' And so he took up a stone. With his head broken, and his eyes full of tears, the monkey looked at the man, and said: 'Oh, do not act thus, sir. You ought rather to restrain others from such deeds.' And without feeling any anger in his mind for this man and without thinking of his pain, he took him to a safe place.

(f) When he was the cobra-king Bhūridatta, he determined to keep the vows of an observance day, and lay down on an ant-hill. A Brahmin then sprinkled his whole body with a juice which burned like the fire which arises at the end of an aeon, put him into a basket and exhibited him throughout the length and breadth of India as a performing snake. But he did not work up the slightest anger even for that Brahmin in his mind. As it is said: 'Although he put me into a basket, and squeezed me tightly with his hands, for Ālambāna I feel no anger, from fear that I might break the moral precepts.'

(g) When he was Campeyya, the cobra-king, he was tormented by a snake-charmer, and yet not the slightest anger rose in his mind. As it is said: 'When at that time I practised the Dharma and kept the vows of the observance day, a snake-charmer took hold of me and displayed me at the palace gate. Whatever colour he might think of, whether blue or yellow or red, adjusting myself to the shifting of his thoughts, I adopted the hue he had thought of. I could change dry land into water, and water into dry land: if I had felt angry towards him, I could instantly have reduced him to ashes. But if I were to exercise this power of my thought, my moral strength would waste away; and once I have lost my moral strength, I would not succeed in winning the highest goal (of Buddhahood).'

(h) When he was Sankhapāla, the cobra-king, sixteen village boys made eight holes in his body with sharp spears, inserted thorny creepers into the holes, passed a tight string through his nose, and carried him along on a pole, while he experienced much pain from his body being dragged along the ground. If he had become angry, he would have had the power to reduce all these village boys to ashes by merely looking at them. But when he actually opened his eyes, he did not show the slightest trace of anger.

(i) And not only these, but many other wonderful deeds he performed, as for instance in the birth story of Mātuposaka, and others.

It is surely most unsuitable and improper that you should allow ill-will to arise in your mind, when you acknowledge as your Teacher that Lord who has won omniscience and who for his practice of the virtue of forbearance has no equal in the whole world, including the Devas.

## 3. WORSHIP

*I. Worship*

1. So as to win this precious thought of Bodhi,
   I now perform the worship of the Buddhas,
   And of the stainless, precious Dharma true,
   And of the Buddha's sons, the oceans of all virtues:
2. All the flowers and all the fruits,
   The healing herbs as many as there are,
   The gems and jewels that adorn this world,
   The waters running so clear and so pleasant,
3. And likewise the jewel-mountains in it,
   The stretches of forest secluded and sweet,
   The creepers resplendent with decorative blossoms,
   The trees with branches bending with fruit,
4. And in the world of the gods the fragrant incenses,
   The wishing trees, and the trees made of jewels,
   The lakes that are covered with lilies
   And resound with the cries of the geese,
5. The harvests which grow without plowman and sower,—
   And all else that may help to adorn the adored,
   And that lies in the spreading sphere of the ether,
   All these things, which in fact are no one's possessions:

6. Them I take up in my mind;—to the best of the Sages
These I present now, to them and their offspring.
May they accept this from me, supremely worthy of gifts,
Greatly compassionate, out of compassion for me.

*II. Salutation*

24. As many times as there are atoms in all Buddha-fields I make obeisance
To all the Buddhas of the triple time, the Dharma, and the best of congregations.

25. All the shrines I salute, and the spots where the Bodhi-being has dwelt,
To the preceptors homage I give, and to holy men worthy of worship.

*III. Taking Refuge*

26. To the Buddha for refuge I go, until the day that Bodhi is won.
To the Dharma for refuge I go, and to the Bodhisattvas great in number.

48. Now, now I go for refuge to the mighty saviours of the world,
The Jinas eager to protect the world, who do remove all fear;

49. To the Dharma they won, which destroys of Samsara the terrors,
With all my heart for refuge I go, and to the Bodhisattvas great in number.

*IV. Confession of Sin*

27. With folded hands I pray to all the Buddhas stationed in all regions,
And likewise to the Bodhisattvas who are great in their compassion:

28. In all my lives without beginning, or in this life now,
Whatever evil I, poor wretch, have done, or caused to be done,

29. Or have approved of, blindly furthering my own harm,
All these offences I confess, and further feel a burning shame about them.

*V. Rejoicing at the Merit of Others*

1. The good works anyone has done, that end the sorrows of the states of woe,
Serenely I rejoice at them : may all the sufferers soon be well!

2. Over the creatures freed from the ills of Samsara, I do rejoice,
And in the Guardians, both in their state of Buddhas-to-be and as Buddhas.

3. Oceanwide their thoughts of Bodhi, bringing ease to all the beings,
Working ceaseless at their welfare,—at the Guides of Bodhi I rejoice.

*VI. Entreaty*

4. All the Buddhas in all regions, I entreat with my hands folded,
May they light the lamp of Dharma, for those lost in suffering's wastes.

*VII. Petition*

5. With folded hands now I petition the Jinas who are ready for Nirvana,
To stay here still for many ages, so that the world may not be struck with blindness.

*VIII. Dedication of Merit*

6. The merit I achieved by all these pious actions, may that make me
Quite able to appease the sufferings of all beings.

7. A medicine for the sick I'll be, their healer, and their servant,
Until the day that sickness is a thing no more remembered.

8. With showers of food and drink I'll quench the pains of hunger and of thirst;
In the dearth at the end of the aeon I'll turn into food and drink.

9. And for the needy I'll be a source of wealth quite unfailing,
Serving them well with all that their needs may require.

*IX. Surrender of Self*

10. Heedless of body, heedless of goods, of the merit I gained and will gain still,
I surrender my all to promote the welfare of others.

*X. Vow to Become a Buddha*

22. As in the past the Blessed Buddhas took the thought of Bodhi,
And passed through all the stages of a Bodhisattva's training in succession,

23. So also I take up the thought of Bodhi for the weal of all,
So also I will train myself on all these stages one by one.

## 4. A NOTE ON VISIONS

In addition to cultivating worship (I 3), the Mahayana also trained its adherents in visions of the Bodhisattvas, and of the Buddhas and their Paradises. Kumarajiva distinguishes three ways in which the Buddha can be seen:

1. Those endowed with supernatural psychic powers may see him with the 'heavenly eye,' hear him with the 'heavenly ear,' and they may fly into the presence of all the Buddhas in all the ten directions.

2. Even those who have no supernatural powers can concentrate their minds on Amida in his Western Paradise, or on other Buddhas.

3. The 'mindfulness of the Buddha-body' concentrates on the body of the Buddha as it is shown in images. Starting with the devout contemplation of an image, the beginner must fix his mind on his forehead. One or more images of the Buddha will then appear on it, depart and then return again. Alternatively, the mind may be fixed on the heart: Buddhas are then seen to issue from it. They hold sceptres of lapis-lazuli, from which rays of light shine forth, and they first depart and then return again. In some cases they issue afterwards by the pores of the skin, and illuminate the entire universe.

The more advanced can perceive, with their spiritual eye, Buddhas multiplied in infinite numbers. Starting from this vision, they then contemplate only the qualities (*guṇa*) of the Buddha, and finally proceed to the Dharma-body, which unites in itself all the qualities of all the numberless Buddhas, and which is similar to space.

These exercises were regarded as precious because they were easier than the traditional ones, and because attachment to sense-objects, the first hindrance precluding traditional trance, offered no insuperable obstacle to them. These visions could be achieved by laymen who had neither attained magical powers nor shed their sense desires. They offered the additional advantage of protection by the Buddha who thinks of his devotee when he thinks of Him with all his might.

These practices, which offered salvation at a cheap price, were, in their more developed form, peculiar to bhaktic Buddhism (see E. Conze, *Buddhism,* chapter 6). To some extent they are nevertheless already foreshadowed in the Scriptures of the Theravadins. During his lifetime the Buddha sometimes projected (*muñcati, pharati*) a radiant, or refulgent, image (*obhāsa*) of himself, with the aim of helping someone in a crisis. Quite a number of examples can be found in the Commentary to the Dhammapada, translated by Burlingame as *Buddhist Legends.* So the Buddha appeared to a monk 'whose *kammaṭṭhāna* had become clear.' 'The apparition brushed the monk's face. Wondering what it was, and looking round, it was as though the Teacher had come and stood there facing him. Rising up, he stretched forth his joined hands in salutation' (Dh-A iii 428). Such an apparition can help the monk to rise by his psychic powers, gained in trance, as if through the air, and to go into the Teacher's presence. Vakkali (iv 118) saw such an apparition of the Teacher, and, 'as though a dry reservoir were flooded with water,' he was filled with rapture and joy. In VM i 228 Mara assumed the shape of the Buddha, and a monk derived such rapture from seeing it that he became an Arahant. On the whole, the importance of all this is, however greatly minimized in the Wisdom tradition of the Theravadins.

## II

# MINDFULNESS

### I. THE MINDFUL AWARENESS OF THE BODY

#### *a. Bodily Postures, Attitudes and Behaviour*

(*A. The four postures*): *When he walks the disciple knows 'I am walking'; when he stands he knows 'I stand,' when he sits he knows 'I sit,' and when he lies down, he knows 'I lie down.' In whichever position his body may be, he knows that it is in that position.*

(*B. Clear comprehension*): *The disciple acts clearly conscious when 1. he sets out (on the alms-round) or returns (from it); 2. looks straight ahead or in other directions; 3. bends and stretches (his limbs); 4. in wearing the garments and carrying the alms-bowl; 5. when he eats, drinks, chews and tastes; 6. discharges excrement and urine; 7. walks, stands, sits; is asleep or awake; talks or keeps silent.*

The commentary (58–98) distinguishes four kinds of clear comprehension:

1. The *purpose* of the action is clearly comprehended as a worthy one. A worthy purpose is one that leads to growth in Dharma. For setting out (B 1) it is therefore a worthy purpose if one travels to visit a shrine, or the elders, or a burial ground (for practising the meditation on the Foul). But with the robe (B 4) one must be mindful to use it only for a permissible purpose, *i.e.*, to keep

out the cold and heat, etc., and similarly with (B 5) food (cf. M. I 10, 'not for sport' etc.). With B 6 the purpose is to avoid discomfort and illness.

2. The surroundings are clearly comprehended as *suitable*. For instance, while it is a good thing to visit a shrine, the multitude of people congregating there may bring harm, temptation, or contact with undesirable things, and in that case the action becomes unsuitable. For B 6 some places are proper, and others are not.

3. In all his actions the disciple continues to keep his mind fixed on one of the 38 subjects of meditation, and does not desert it. This is called the clear comprehension of the monk's proper sphere (*gocara*). He ought to carry his chosen subject about with him all the time. When walking 'he should not raise his foot with a mind bereft of the subject of meditation. But if he has done so, he retraces his step, and repeats it once more.'

4. The clear comprehension which is expressive of *non-delusion*. This is directed against the personalist interpretation with which we usually invest our actions. 'The monk, when he moves forwards or backwards, is not like a blind worldling who in his delusion thinks that it is a self which moves, or that the movement has been produced by a self, as when one says, "I go forwards," or "the act of going forwards is produced by me." But, free from delusion, he thinks: "when there arises in the mind the idea 'I will move forward,' then there arises also, together with just that idea, a nervous impulse (lit. a process of oscillation, *vāyodhātu*), which originates from the mind and generates bodily expression." It is thus that this heap of bones, which is politely called a "body," moves forwards, as a result of the diffusion of a nervous impulse due to the mind. Who then is there the one who walks? To whom does this walking belong? In the ultimate sense it is the going of impersonal physical pro-

cesses (lit. "elements"), and it is also their standing, sitting and lying down.'

The commentary, observing that the postures occur three times, states (no. 95) that the first time (A) the text refers to postures of long duration, the second time (B 1 and 3) to those of middle duration, and the third time (B 7) to those of brief duration. As for the latter: 'If somebody, after walking about or walking hither and thither for some time, then stands still and reflects, "the mental and physical processes which proceeded at the time of walking have now stopped,"—then he is one who is clearly conscious of walking. He is one who is clearly conscious of standing if, after he has stood still for some time, either memorizing (the holy texts) or attending to a subject of meditation, he then sits down and reflects, "the mental and physical processes which proceeded at the time of standing have now stopped." He is one who is clearly conscious of sitting if, after he has sat down for some time, reciting the holy texts, and so on, he then lies down and reflects, "the mental and physical processes which proceeded at the time of sitting have now stopped." Again, someone is clearly conscious of being asleep or awake if, after lying on his back for some time, reciting the holy texts or attending to a subject of meditation, he has fallen asleep, and after that, on waking, he reflects, "the mental and physical processes which proceeded at the time of sleeping have now stopped." When action-producing thoughts do not proceed one speaks of "sleep"; when they do, of "being awake." Someone talks mindfully and clearly conscious if, when talking, he thinks, "this sound has been born dependent on the lips, teeth, tongue, palate, and the effort of thought conforming to that sound." He is called one who is a clearly conscious agent in talking if, after he has for some time recited the holy texts, or preached the

Dharma, or spoken aloud the formula of his meditation, or answered questions, later, on falling silent, he reflects, "the mental and physical processes which arose at the time of talking have now stopped." Finally, somebody is said to practise the clear comprehension of keeping silent if, after attending to the Dharma or his meditation, he has kept silent for some time, and then afterwards he reflects that "the mental and physical processes which proceeded at the time of keeping silent have now stopped; one speaks of 'talking' where there is a proceeding of (certain) derivative (as distinct from primary, elemental) material processes; where that is absent one speaks of 'keeping silent' ".'

### *b. Breathing Mindfulness*

(*Posture*): The Lord has said that the disciple should *'sit down,'* so as to indicate a posture which is calm, and which does not lead to either slackness or restlessness. He adds that he should *'sit cross-legged,'* because this position is firm, easy for in-breathing and out-breathing, and expedient for seizing the object. *'Keeping the body straight,'*—the disciple holds the upper part of his body upright, brings the 18 vertebrae from beginning to end into a straight line. Then his skin, muscles and sinews are not cramped. And those sensations do not arise which might come up any moment if they were cramped. His mind can therefore become one-pointed, and his meditational practice does not come to naught, but grows and increases.

(*Attentiveness to breathing*): 'Mindfully he breathes in, mindfully he breathes out.' (The Scripture then enumerates 16 ways in which mindful breathing should be practised. These are the first four, suitable to the beginner:)

'1. Breathing out a long breath, he knows, "I breathe out a long breath"; breathing in a long breath, he knows, "I breathe in a long breath."

2. Breathing out a short breath, etc., as at 1.

3. Experiencing the whole breath-body I will breathe out, so he trains himself; experiencing the whole breath-body I will breathe in, so he trains himself.

4. Calming down the functions of the body I will breathe out, so he trains himself; calming down the functions of the body I will breathe in, so he trains himself.'

(*1. Counting*): The son of good family, who is still a beginner, should attend to this meditation first of all by way of counting (the breaths). In counting he should not stop short of 5, nor go beyond 10, and there should be no interruption (of the counting; or gap in the series, *e.g.*, 1, 2, 5, 7). For, if he stops short of 5, the thought produced in that confined space of time becomes agitated, like a herd of cows shut up in a confined cow-pen. But if he goes beyond 10, the thought is produced with only the counting (and not the breath) for its basis. If, however, he allows a gap or interruption to take place, his thought will waver, wondering whether the meditation will reach completion or not. Therefore when counting one should avoid these faults. He should count in such a way that he seizes on the breathing in and out as they come up, and notes each one as it takes place, beginning with '1, 1,' up to '10, 10' (when he can again begin with 1). And when he counts in this way, the breathings in and the breathings out become obvious as they stream in and as they stream out. He comes to know that they pass along again and again, but he should not seize on them either inside or outside (the body), but only at the point where they reach the nostril. In this meditation connected with counting the mind becomes one-pointed just by the force of the counting, as a ship is held still in a swift current when a firm hold is kept on the rudder.

And for how long should one go on counting? Until, without counting, mindfulness is established in the breathing in and out as its object. For counting has no other purpose than to cut off the discursive thinking which chases after external objects, and to establish mindfulness in the in-breathings and out-breathings as its object.

(2. *Pursuing*): Next he should attend by pursuing. The word 'pursuing' means that, after counting has been given up the in-breathings and out-breathings are without interruption pursued with mindfulness. But that does not mean that the breath should be pursued up to its beginning, middle, or end. Of the outgoing breath the navel is the beginning, the heart the middle, the nose the end. Of the incoming breath the nose-tip is the beginning, the heart the middle, and the navel the end. If someone tries to follow it (all that way), his mind, distracted, will be thrown into turmoil and unrestful wavering. Therefore, when he attends (to the breath) by pursuing it, he should not attend to it by way of beginning, middle, and end. But he should pay attention to the place where the breath touches the nostril, and persevere in this until full concentration is attained. This is illustrated by the simile of the saw: Suppose that a tree trunk were laid on to level ground, and a man were to cut it with a saw. The man's attention is then directed on those teeth of the saw which come into contact with the tree trunk, but he pays no attention to them as they advance or recede, and yet he is not unaware of the fact that they do so.

(*3. The mental image*): To some people who attend to this meditation, the mental image appears before long, and they achieve the full concentration which is equipped with the remaining Jhana-limbs.

In the case of others, again, subsequent to the time of their attending by way of counting, as the distress of their body is more and more appeased by the gradual stopping of their coarser in-breathings and out-breathings, both their body and their thought become light, as if their body would want to jump up into the air. When the coarser breathings have quite stopped, thought proceeds with the mental image of the subtle breathings as its object. When these also have stopped, the mental image of the object becomes increasingly more and more subtle. How? It is as if a man were to strike a bronze gong with a big bronze gong-stick; at one single stroke a loud sound would arise, and the man's thought would proceed with the coarse sound for its object. But when the coarse sound has stopped, there is after that the object which consists in the mental image of the finer tones; and, when that also has stopped, the mental image of the sound-object becomes increasingly more and more subtle. The object of the other meditations becomes more distinct on the higher stages, but it is not so with this one. As one develops it higher and higher, it becomes more and more subtle (and elusive), and does not stand out at all clearly. It is for this reason that the Lord has said (S v 337): 'I do not, oh monks, teach the development of breathing-mindfulness for one who is deprived of mindfulness, and who cannot be clearly conscious (of what he does).' For although all meditations can be achieved only by those who are mindful and clearly conscious, yet in the case of all the others, except this one, the object becomes clearer with repeated attention. But this meditation of the breathing-mindfulness is difficult, hard to develop, and forms a proper object of attention only for great men, such as Buddhas, Pratyekabuddhas, and Sons (Disciples) of the Buddhas. It is not a trivial thing, and it cannot be cultivated by trivial people. The more one pays attention to it, the more it becomes calm, subtle (and elusive). Therefore it requires powerful mindfulness and strong wisdom.

When practice is continued in this manner, before long the mental image will appear. But this is not the same for all. To some it appears like something which lightly touches (the skin), such as cotton-wool, or silk-cotton, or a breeze. That is what some say. But this is the decision of the Commentaries: This image appears to some in the form of a star, or a cluster of jewels, or a cluster of pearls; to others like something which has a harsh touch, like a cotton seed, or a needle made of hard-wood; to others like a long string, a garland of flowers, a column of smoke; to others like a drawn out spider's thread, a (filmy) mass of clouds, a lotus flower, a chariot wheel, the disk of the moon, or the disk of the sun. And the matter here is like this: When a number of monks sit together, and a Sutra has been recited, some monk may ask, 'How does this Sutra appear to you?' Then one may reply, 'It appears to me like a mighty mountain river,' another 'to me like a line of trees', another, 'to me like a tree which is laden with fruits, has plenty of branches, and gives a cool shade.' For one and the same Sutra appears different to them because of the difference of their imagination (lit. 'perception'). Just so this one subject of meditation appears different to different imaginations. For it is born of imagination, founded on imagination, sprung from imagination.

(*4. Access*): From the appearance of the mental image onwards the hindrances are impeded, the defiling passions are subdued, mindfulness is set up, and thought is concentrated by access-concentration.

(*Advantages*): This breathing-mindfulness brings great fruit and advantage. Its great advantage should be known from the fact that it results in a state of calm, etc., according to the statement that 'this concentration on breathing-mindfulness, oh monks, when developed and made much of, is calm and sublime' (S v 321), and so on. In addition it is capable of cutting off discursive thinking. For, owing to the fact that it is calm, sublime, unblemished and conducive to well-being, it prevents thought from roaming about here and there with its discursive thinking, which acts as an obstacle to transic concentration, and it brings the mind face to face with breathing as its object.

## 2. THE MINDFUL AWARENESS OF MENTAL PROCESSES

### *a. Feelings*

(*The canonical text*): *Here the disciple, feeling a pleasant feeling, knows 'I feel a pleasant feeling.' And so with: unpleasant feelings; neither pleasant nor unpleasant feelings; worldly pleasant, unpleasant, neither pleasant nor unpleasant feelings; unworldly (spiritual) pleasant, unpleasant, neither pleasant nor unpleasant feelings.*

The meaning is: When he feels a *pleasant* feeling, physical or mental, the disciple comprehends that he feels a pleasant feeling. It is true that even infants who still lie on their backs, at the time when they drink their mother's milk, and so on, comprehend that they feel pleasure when they feel pleasure. But here this kind of knowledge is not meant. For that does not forsake the apprehension of a (living) being, does not remove the notion of a being, and it does not involve an act of meditation, or a development of the applications of mindfulness. But the knowledge of this monk forsakes the apprehension of a being, removes the notion of a being, and it is an act of meditation and a development of the pillars of mindfulness.

What is meant here is an act of cognition which knows clearly what feels, what has the feeling, and for what reason the feeling takes place. What is it then that feels? Not any being or person. What has the feeling? Not any being or person. For what reason does the feeling take place? Feelings arise with objects (*i.e.*, forms, sounds, smells, tastes, touchables and mind-objects) as their basis. The disciple therefore comprehends that, having made this or that object a basis for (feelings that are) pleasurable, and so on, he experiences a feeling. But when, on account of that feeling occuring, he thinks 'I am feeling,' that is merely a conventional expression.

When a pleasant or an unpleasant feeling arises, the fact is quite obvious. But when a feeling arises which is *neither pleasant nor unpleasant,* the fact is hard to discern, obscure, and not at all clear. It becomes obvious when one takes hold of it by inference: 'The feeling which is neither pleasant nor unpleasant is to be found on the occasion of the disappearance of the pleasant or unpleasant feeling, in a middle position between the two, as contrary to both the agreeable and the disagreeable (feeling).' What could it be compared to? A hunter follows the hoofmarks of a deer which has fled across a flat rocky ridge. When he sees the hoofmarks on both sides of the rocky ridge, but sees none in the middle between the two, then he knows by inference that here the deer went up, there it went down, and in the middle, on the flat rocky ridge, it must have gone along this line: When a pleasant feeling arises, it becomes obvious like the hoofmarks in the place where the deer went up. When an unpleasant feeling arises, it becomes obvious like the hoofmarks in the place where it went down. But a feeling which is neither pleasant nor unpleasant becomes obvious when one takes hold of it by inference, *i.e.*, on the occasion of the disappearance of the pleasant or unpleasant feeling, in a middle position between the two, as contrary to both agreeable and disagreeable feelings, and it is like the inference that the deer has gone across here in the middle (over that rocky ridge).

There is still another method by which one can understand (feelings mindfully): The disciple wisely knows 'I feel a pleasant feeling' because, when he feels a pleasant feeling, the unpleasant feeling is absent at the moment of the pleasant feeling being felt. And he becomes clearly aware of the fact that this feeling is impermanent, does not last, is doomed to reversal, because the unpleasant feelings which preceded it are absent from it, and this pleasant feeling itself did formerly not exist. And so for the unpleasant feelings, and those which are neither pleasant nor unpleasant. As the Lord has said (M i 500): 'Pleasant, unpleasant, or neutral feeling, Aggivessana, is indeed impermanent, compounded, brought about by conditioned co-production, doomed to extinction, doomed to break up, fit for dispassion, fit for cessation. When the learned and holy disciple sees this, he turns away from all feelings, be they pleasant, unpleasant, or neutral; he loses his greed for them, is freed from them, and has a cognition of the fact that he is freed from them.'

### *b. The five hindrances*

(*The canonical text*): *Here the disciple dwells with re-*

*gard to dharmas in the contemplation of dharmas,—and in the first place with regard to the five hindrances.*

*I 1. He knows of the existing inward sense-desire that 'There is to me inward sense-desire.'*
*I 2. Of the non-existing inward sense-desire he knows that 'there is not to me inward sense-desire.'*
*I 3. And how of the unproduced sense-desire the production takes place, also that he knows.*
*I 4. And how of the produced sense-desire the forsaking takes place, also that he knows.*
*I 5. And how of the forsaken sense-desire there is no production in the future, that also he knows.*
The same formula with:

II 1–5. Ill-will.
III 1–5. Sloth and torpor.
IV 1–5. Excitedness and sense of guilt.
V 1–5. Indecision.

I–V, 1–2. *Existing* means that which exists by way of repeated habitual behaviour. *Non-existing* means that which does not exist by way of habitual behaviour, or because it has been forsaken.

I 3. The production of *sense-desire* is due to unwise attention to the sign of what seems attractive. Unwise attention is inexpedient attention, attention on the wrong track, attention which mistakes the impermanent for the permanent, ill for ease, not-self for self, the repulsive for the attractive. Sense-desire arises when that kind of attention proceeds abundantly with regard to an attractive object.

I 4. It is forsaken by means of wise attention to something which is unattractive. And wise attention is expedient attention, attention on the right track, attention which sees the impermanent as impermanent, ill as ill, not-self as not-self, the unattractive as unattractive. Sense-desire is forsaken when that kind of attention proceeds abundantly with regard to such an object.

And six dharmas are conducive to the forsaking of sense-desire. They are:

1. The contemplation of the ten kinds of repulsiveness, as seen in the corpses of men and animals (see II 5c).

2. Devotion to the development of meditation on that which is unattractive (see II 5a–b).

3. The guarding of the doors of the senses (see II 3a).

4. Moderation in eating.

5. The company of good men who work on this kind of meditation and delight in it.

6. Suitable talk, *i.e.*, whether standing or sitting one discusses problems connected with the tenfold contemplation of the Foul.

I 5. Finally the disciple knows that the future (definite) non-production of the sense-desire which has been forsaken by these six dharmas will take place on the Path of Arhatship.

II 3. The production of *ill-will* is due to unwise attention to the sign of what seems offensive . . . (etc. as at I 3).

II 4. It is forsaken by means of wise attention to the liberation of the heart through friendliness.

And six dharmas are conducive to the forsaking of ill-will:

1. To take up the contemplation of friendliness. For ill-will is forsaken even in one who only takes up the meditation on friendliness, when he but diffuses friendliness to particular persons, or in general, or in the ten directions (see III 2b, pp. 130–1).

2. Devotion to the development of the meditation on friendliness, whether it be diffused with differentiations, or in general, or in the ten directions (see III 2b).

3. Reflections on the fact that beings are the product of their own deeds. The disciple should reflect on the fact that both he and his foe are made by their own karma as follows: 'What can you do to him now that you are so angry with him? Will you be able to destroy his morality, and other virtues? Have you not come here as a result of your own deeds, and will the manner of your going away not also be determined by your own deeds? To get angry with somebody else is like wanting to hit others with glowing coals, red-hot crowbars, excrement etc., after one has taken them into one's hands.' 'And he also, who is so angry, what can he do to you? Can he destroy your morality, or other virtues? He also has come here as a result of his own deeds, and the manner of his going away is likewise determined by his own deeds. Let this wrath of his be like a present which is not accepted; let it be like a handful of dust thrown against the wind; it will only fall on his own head' (see p. 122).

4. The abiding in the abundance of such considerations (as at 3).

5. The company of good men who delight in the development of the meditation on friendliness.

6. Suitable talk, *i.e.*, concerning the problems of the meditation on friendliness.

II 5. Finally he knows that the future (definite) non-production of the ill-will which has been forsaken by these six dharmas will take place on the Path of a Never-returner.

III 3. The production of *sloth and torpor* is due to unwise attention to discontent, and kindred conditions (enumerated at S v 103). It is due to: (a) 'Discontent,' which means annoyance; (b) lassitude, which means bodily laziness; (c) 'languidity,' which means that one is torpid in one's bodily movements, when getting up, etc.; (d) 'lethargy after a meal,' which means the feeling of faintness or discomfort which may follow a meal; (e) 'mental sluggishness,' which means that the mind is in a sluggish state.

III 4. It is, however, forsaken by means of wise attention to the three stages of vigorous effort. The first of these is vigour at its inception, in other words vigour in its initial stages; the second is continued exertion, which is more powerful, having left indolence behind; the third, progressive endeavour, is still more powerful, attacking one goal after another.

And six dharmas are conducive to the forsaking of sloth and torpor:

1. Excessive eating is seen as a reason for sloth and torpor.

2. A posture which induces sloth and torpor is exchanged for another one which does not.

3. One is attentive to the perception of light, *i.e.*, by night one pays attention to the light of the moon, of a lamp, of a torch, and by day to that of the sun.

4. Dwelling in open places.

5. The cultivation of good men who have forsaken sloth and torpor.

6. Suitable talk, *i.e.*, concerning the ascetic practices.

III 5. Finally he knows that the future (definite) non-production of the sloth and torpor which has been forsaken by these six dharmas will take place on the Path of an Arhat.

IV 3. The production of *excitedness and sense of guilt* is due to unwise attention to mental disquietude.

IV 4. It is, however, forsaken by means of wise attention to the mental quietude which is defined as transic concentration.

And six dharmas are conducive to the forsaking of excitedness and sense of guilt:

1. The acquisition of great learning: One learns, one, two, three, four or five collections of the Scriptures, both the words and the meaning of them.

2. The asking of many questions, about what is proper and what is not.

3. To be versed in the regulations of the Vinaya, and to master them.

4. The cultivation of elders, *i.e.*, one approaches old and venerable Theras.

5. The cultivation of good men who are experts in the Vinaya.

6. Suitable talk, *i.e.*, concerning that which is proper and that which is not.

IV 5. Finally he knows, with regard to the future (definite) non-production of the excitedness and sense of guilt which have been forsaken by these six dharmas, that for excitedness it will take place on the Path of an Arhat, and for the sense of guilt on that of a Never-returner.

V 3. The production of indecision is due to unwise attention to dharmas which again and again cause indecision and doubt.

V 4. It is, however, forsaken by means of wise attention to dharmas which are (clearly distinguished as) wholesome or unwholesome, faulty or faultless, to be cultivated or not to be cultivated, low or exalted, appertaining to darkness or light.

And six dharmas are conducive to the forsaking of indecision:

1. The acquisition of great learning (as at IV).

2. The asking of many questions, about the Three Treasures.

3. Understanding the nature of the Vinaya (as at IV).

4. An abundance of resolute faith, defined as the faith which is willing to put its trust in the Three Treasures.

5. The cultivation of good men who are intent on faith.

6. Suitable talk, *i.e.*, concerning the virtues (qualities) of the Three Treasures.

V 5. Finally he knows that the future (definite) non-production of the indecision which has been forsaken by these six dharmas takes place on the Path of a Stream-winner.

### 3. THE REPUDIATION OF THE SENSORY WORLD

#### *a. Guarding (restraint of) the senses*

This is the morality which consists in the restraint of the senses: *'Here someone, 1. having seen a form with his eye, does not seize on its general appearance, or the (accessory) details of it. That which might, so long as he dwells unrestrained as to the (controlling) force of the eye, give occasion for covetous, sad, evil and unwholesome dharmas to flood him, that he sets himself to restrain; he guards the controlling force of the eye, and brings about its restraint. And likewise 2. when he has heard sounds with the ear, 3. smelled smells with the nose, 4. tasted tastes with the tongue, 5. touched touchables with the body, 6. cognized mind-objects (dharmas) with the mind'* (M i. 180).

*Having seen a form with his eye,*—when he has seen a form with the visual consciousness which is capable of seeing forms, and which in normal language is usually called the 'eye,' though it actually is its tool. For the Ancients have said: 'The eye cannot see forms because it is without thought; thought cannot see forms, because it is without eye. When the object knocks against the door (of sight) one sees with the thought which has eye-sensibility for its basis. In the expression "one sees with the eye," only an accessory equipment is indicated just as one may say, "one shoots with a bow" (and not, "with an arrow"). Therefore the meaning here is: 'having seen form with visual consciousness.'

*He does not seize on its general appearance* (lit. 'the sign')—he does not seize on its appearance as man or woman, or its appearance as attractive, etc. which makes it into a basis for the defiling passions. But he stops at what is actually seen. *He does not seize on the details of it,*—he does not seize on the variety of its accessory features, like the hands or feet, the smile, the laughter, the talk, the looking here, the looking away, etc., which are in common parlance called 'details' (*anubyañjana*) because they manifest the defiling passions, by again and again (*anu anu*) tainting with them (*byañjanato*). But he seizes only on that which is really there, (*i.e.,* the impurity of the 32 parts of the body; see II 5a). Like Mahātissa, the Elder, who lived on Mount Cetiya. Once that Thera went from Mount Cetiya to Anurādhapura, to gather alms. In a certain family the daughter-in-law had quarrelled with her husband, and, adorned and beautified like a heavenly maiden, she left Anurādhapura early in the morning, and went away to stay with some relatives. On the way she saw the Thera, and, as her mind was perverted, she gave a loud laugh. The Thera looked to see what was the matter; he acquired at the sight of her teeth (-bones) the notion of repulsiveness (impurity), and thereby reached Arhatship. . . . The husband who ran after her on the same road, saw the Thera, and asked him whether he had by any chance seen a woman. The Thera replied:

'Whether what went along here
Was a man or a woman, I do not know.
But a collection of bones is moving
Now along this main road.'

*That which might,* etc.: that might be the reason, or that non-restraint of the faculty of the eye might be the cause, why in this person,—when he *dwells* without having restrained the faculty of the eye with the gate of mindfulness, i.e., when he has left the door of the eye open,—such dharmas as covetousness, etc., *flood* him, *i.e.*, pursue and submerge him. *That he sets himself to restrain,*—he sets himself to close this faculty of the eye with the gate of mindfulness. And one who sets himself to do that, of him it is said that *he guards the controlling force of the eye, and brings about its restraint.*

But it is not with reference to the faculty of the eye itself that there is restraint or non-restraint (*i.e.*, it does not apply to the initial stage of the impact of the stimulus on the eye), and it is not concerning the eye considered as a sensitive organ that mindfulness arises, or the lack of it. But it is at (the stage of the apperception of the object, with such and such a meaning and significance, and the volitional reaction to it, which is technically known as) the 'impulsive moment,' that there is lack of restraint, if and when immorality arises then, or lack of mindfulness, or lack of cognition, lack of patience or laziness. Nevertheless one speaks of the non-restraint of the sense of sight. And why? Because when the mind is in that condition, also the door (of the eye) is unguarded. The situation can be compared with that of a city: when its four gates are unguarded, then, although in the interior of the city the doors of the houses, the store-rooms and private rooms are well guarded, nevertheless all the property in the city is actually unguarded and unprotected, and robbers can, once they have entered through the city-gates, do whatever they like. In the same sense also the door (of the eye) is unguarded when, in consequence of the arising of immorality, etc., there is lack of restraint at the 'impulsive moment.'

But when morality, etc., arise at that moment, then the door (of sight) also is guarded. Just again as with the city: When the city-gates are well guarded, then, although in the interior the doors of the houses, etc., are unguarded, nevertheless all the property in the city is actually well guarded and well protected; for, the city-gates being closed, robbers cannot enter. Just so also the door (of the eye) is guarded when morality, etc., arise at the 'impulsive moment.'

The same explanation applies to: *when he has heard sounds with the ear,* etc. The restraint of the senses thus consists, in short, in the avoiding of the seizing on the general appearance, etc., of sight-objects, etc., which lead to one's being pursued by the defiling passions.

And it should be achieved through mindfulness. For it is effected by mindfulness, in so far as the sense-organs, when they are governed by mindfulness, can no longer be influenced by covetousness, etc. Therefore we should remember the 'Fire-Sermon' (S iv 168) which says: 'It were better, oh monks, if the eye were stroked with a heated iron bar, afire, ablaze, aflame, than that one should seize on either the general appearance or the details of the forms of which the eye is aware.' The disciple should achieve a thorough restraint of the senses, in that, by means of unimpaired mindfulness, he prevents that seizing on the general appearance, etc., which makes the consciousness, which proceeds through the door of the eye, etc., with forms, etc., for its range (province), liable to be flooded (influenced) by covetousness, etc.

And one should become like Cittagutta, the Elder, who lived in the great Kurandaka Cave. In that cave there was a delightful painting which showed the seven Buddhas leaving for the homeless life. One day numerous monks were wandering about in the cave, going from lodging to lodging. They noticed the painting, and said: 'What a delightful painting, Venerable Bhikkhu!' The Thera replied: 'For more than 60 years, brethren, I have lived in this cave, and I have never known whether there is a painting here or whether there is not. To-day only I have learned it from you people, who use your eyes.' For all that time during which the Thera had lived there, he had never lifted up his eyes, and looked more closely at the cave. At the entrance to the cave there was a large ironwood tree. To that also the Thera had never looked up; but he knew that it was in flower when each year he saw the filaments which had fallen down on the ground.

All the sons of good family who have their own welfare at heart should therefore remember:

'Let not the eye wander like forest ape,
Or trembling wood deer, or affrighted child.
The eyes should be cast downwards; they should look
The distance of a yoke; he shall not serve
His thought's dominion, like a restless ape.'

### b. The control of the mind

*The Sutra on the composition of ideas:*

*If, whilst attending to a certain sign, there arise, with reference to it, in the disciple evil and unwholesome ideas, connected with greed, hate or delusion, then the disciple*

*I. should, by means of this sign (=cause, occasion) attend to another sign, which is more wholesome;*

*II. or he should investigate the peril of these ideas: 'Unwholesome truly are these ideas! Blameworthy are these ideas! Of painful result are these ideas!';*

*III. or he should pay no attention to these ideas;*

*IV. or he should attend to the composition of the factors which effect these ideas;*

*V. or, with teeth clenched and tongue pressed against the gums, he should by means of sheer mental effort hold back, crush and burn out the (offending) thought;*

*in doing so, these evil and unwholesome ideas, bound up with greed, hate or delusion, will be forsaken and disappear; from their forsaking thought will become inwardly settled and calm, composed and concentrated. This is called the effort to overcome.*

The *commentary* says:

I. Unwholesome ideas may arise with reference to beings,—be they desirable, undesirable, or unconsidered,—or to things, such as one's possessions, or things which annoy, like stumps or thorns. The wholesome counter-ideas which drive them out arise from the following practices, which are directly opposed to them:

Greed about beings: Meditation about the repulsiveness of the body.

About things: Attention to their impermanence.

Hate for beings: The development of friendliness.

For things: Attention to the elements: which of

the physical elements composing the thing am I angry with? (cf. p. 125).

Delusion about both beings and things:

1. When he has, in his general bewilderment, neglected his duties to a teacher, he wakes himself up by doing some tiresome work, such as carrying water.
2. When he has been hazy in attending to the teacher's explanation of the doctrine, he wakes himself up by doing some tiresome work.
3. He removes his doubts by questioning authorities.
4. At the right time he listens respectfully to the Dharma.
5. He acquires the skill in distinguishing between correct and faulty conclusions, and knows that 'this is the reason for that, this is not the reason.'

These are the direct and correct antidotes to the faulty ideas.

II. He investigates them with the power of wisdom, and rejects them like a snake's carcass.

III. 'He should not remember those ideas, not attend to them, but become one who is otherwise engaged. He should be like someone who, not wanting to see a certain sight-object, just closes his eyes; when these ideas arise in his mind, he should take hold of his basic subject of meditation, and become engaged on that.' It may help him to break the spell of intruding thoughts and to occupy his mind otherwise, if he recites with great faith a passage from the Scriptures, or reads out a passage in praise of the Buddha or Dharma; or he may sort out his belongings, and enumerate them one by one, 'these are the scissors,' 'this is the needle,' etc.; or he should do some sewing; or he should do some good work for a given period of time. And after that he should return to his basic subject of meditation.

IV. He should analyse the conditions for these ideas and ask himself: 'What is their cause, what their condition, what the reason for their having arisen?'

V. He should put forth great vigour, and with a wholesome thought he should hold back an unwholesome one.

### *c. Similes for the evils of sense-desires*

23. Whether they seek them or have them, men always
 thirst for more;
 Unless they let them go, suffering is sure to ensue.
 Since, like a lighted torch of grass, they burn the
 hand,
 Who, self-possessed, would take delight in sense-
 desires?
24. The uncontrolled whom they have bitten in their
 hearts,
 Go to destruction and by no means bliss obtain.
 Since they can be compared to fierce and raging
 serpents,
 Who, self-possessed, would take delight in sense-
 desires?
25. It is as with a hungry dog who gnaws a bone;
 Though tasted, never give they satisfaction.
 Since they are thus a mass of dry, old bones
 Who, self-possessed, would take delight in sense-
 desires?
26. Their objects shared with kings, thieves, fire and
 water,
 Nothing but ill can possibly result from them.
 Since they are thus just like a bait exposed,
 Who, self-possessed, would take delight in sense-
 desires?

27. To those that tend them there is much misfortune,
From foes as well as from their own relations.
Since thus their range is haunted by great dangers,
Who, self-possessed, would take delight in sense-desires?

28. Those men who reach for them on mountains or in forests,
In rivers or the ocean, thereby often come to grief.
Since they are like the topmost fruits that hang on trees,
Who, self-possessed, would take delight in sense-desires?

29. Gained at the price of many bitter efforts,
They are destroyed here often in a moment.
Since thus they are mere dream-enjoyments,
Who, self-possessed, would take delight in sense-desires?

## 4. THE RECOLLECTION OF DEATH

In 'the recollection of death,' the word 'death' refers to the cutting off of the life-force which lasts for the length of one existence. Whoso wants to develop it, should in seclusion and solitude wisely set up attention with the words: 'Death will take place, the life-force will be cut off,' or (simply), 'Death, death.' But if somebody takes up an unwise attitude (to this problem of death), then sorrow will arise in him when he recalls the death of a loved person, like the grief of a mother when she thinks of the death of the dear child whom she has borne; and joy will arise when he recalls the death of an unloved person, like the rejoicing of a foe who thinks of an enemy's death; and when he recalls the death of an indifferent person, no perturbation will arise in him, just as the man who all day long burns corpses looks on dead bodies without perturbation; when, finally, he recalls his own death, violent trembling arises in him, as in a frightened man who sees before him a murderer with his sword drawn. And all this is the result of a lack in mindfulness, (reasonable) perturbation and cognition.

Therefore the Yogin should look upon beings killed or dead here and there, and advert to the death of beings who died after having first seen prosperity. To this (observation) he should apply mindfulness, perturbation and cognition, and set up attention with the words, 'Death will take place,' and so on. When he proceeds thus, he proceeds wisely, *i.e.,* he proceeds expediently. For only if someone proceeds in this way will his hindrances be impeded, will mindfulness be established with death for its object, and will some degree of concentration be achieved.[1]

If this is not enough (to produce access), he should recall death from the following eight points of view:

1. as a murderer, standing in front of him;
2. from the (inevitable) loss of (all) achievement;
3. by inference;
4. because one's body is shared with many others;
5. from the weakness of the stuff of life;
6. from the absence of signs;
7. because the life-span is limited;
8. from the shortness of the moment.

1. *'As a murderer standing in front of him,'* means, 'as if a murderer were standing in front of him.' One should recall that death stands in front of us just like a murderer, who confronts us with his drawn sword raised to our neck, intending to cut off our head. And why? Be-

[1]Literally: 'will the subject of meditation attain to access.'

cause death comes together with birth, and deprives us of life.

(a) As a budding mushroom shoots upwards carrying soil on its head, so beings from their birth onwards carry decay and death along with them. For death has come together with birth, because everyone who is born must certainly die. Therefore this being, from the time of his birth onwards, moves in the direction of death, without turning back even for a moment; (b) just as the sun, once it has arisen, goes forward in the direction of its setting, and does not turn back for a moment on the path it traverses in that direction; (c) or as a mountain stream rapidly tears down on its way, flows and rushes along, without turning back even for a moment. To one who goes along like that, death is always near; (d) just as brooks get extinguished when dried up by the summer heat; (e) as fruits are bound to fall from a tree early one day when their stalks have been rotted away by the early morning mists; (f) as earthenware breaks when hit with a hammer; (g) and as dewdrops are dispersed when touched by the rays of the sun. Thus death, like a murderer with a drawn sword has come together with birth. Like the murderer who has raised his sword to our neck, so it deprives us of life. And there is no chance that it will desist.

2. *'By the failure of achievement,'*—which means: Here in this world achievement prospers only so long as it is not overwhelmed by failure. And there is no single achievement that stands out as having transcended the (threat of) failure.

Moreover, all health ends in sickness, all youth in old age, all life in death; wherever one may dwell in the world, one is afflicted by birth, overtaken by old age, oppressed by sickness, struck down by death. Through realizing that the achievements of life thus end in the failure of death, he should recollect death from the failure of achievement.

3. *'By inference,'* means that one draws an inference for oneself from others. And it is with seven kinds of person that one should compare oneself: those great in fame, great in merit, great in might, great in magical power, great in wisdom, Pratyekabuddhas, and fully enlightened Buddhas.

In what manner? This death has assuredly befallen even those (kings) like Mahāsammata, Mandhātu, Mahāsudassana, Dalhanemin and Nimippabhūti, who possessed great fame, a great retinue, and who abounded in treasures and might. How then could it be that it will not befall also me?

'The greatly famous, noble kings,
Like Mahāsammata and others,
They all fell down before the might of death.
What need is there to speak of men like us?'

(And so for the other six kinds of distinction.)

In this way he draws from others, who have achieved great fame, and so on, an inference as to himself, *i.e.*, that death is common to himself and to them. When he recalls that, 'as for those distinguished beings so also for me death will take place,' then the subject of meditation attains to access.

4. *'Because one's body is shared with many others'*: this body is the common property of many. It is shared by the eighty classes of parasitic animals, and it incurs death as a result of their turbulence. Likewise it belongs to the many hundreds of diseases which arise within it, as well as to the outside occasions of death, such as snakes, scorpions, and so on.

For just as, flying from all directions, arrows, spears,

lances, stones, and so on, fall on a target placed at the cross roads, so on the body also all kinds of misfortune are bound to descend. And through the onslaught of these misfortunes it incurs death. Hence the Lord has said: 'Here, monks, a monk, when the day is over and night comes round, thinks to himself: many are, to be sure, for me the occasions of death: a snake, or a scorpion, or a centipede may bite me; thereby I may lose my life, and that may act as an obstacle (to my spiritual progress). Or I may stumble and fall, or the food I have eaten may upset me, or the bile may trouble me, or the phlegm, or the winds which cut like knives; and thereby I may lose my life, and that may act as an obstacle' (A III 306).

5. *'From the weakness of the stuff of life'*:—this life-force is without strength and feeble. For the life of beings is bound up with (a) breathing in and out, (b) the postures, (c) heat and cold, (d) the (four) great primaries, and (e) with food.

(a) It goes on only as long as it can obtain an even functioning of breathing in and out; as soon, however, as air issues from the nose without re-entering, or enters without going out again, one is considered dead. (b) Again, it goes on only as long as it can obtain an even functioning of the four postures: but through the preponderance of one or the other of these the vital activities are cut off. (c) Again, it goes on as long as it can obtain the even functioning of heat and cold; but it fails when oppressed by excessive heat or cold. (d) Again, it goes on as long as it can obtain the even functioning of the (four) great primaries; but through the disturbance of one or the other of them, (*i.e.*) of the solid, fluid, etc., element, the life of even a strong person is extinguished, be it by the stiffening of his body, or because his body has become wet and putrid from dysentery, and so on, or because it is overcome by a high temperature, or because his sinews are torn. (e) Again, life goes on only as long as one obtains solid food, at suitable times; when one cannot get food, it gets extinguished.

6. *'From the absence of signs,'*—because one cannot determine (the time of death, etc.). 'From the absence of a definite limit,' that is the meaning. For one says with regard to the death of beings:

(a) Life's duration, (b) sickness, (c) time,
(d) The place where the body is cast off, (e) the future destiny,
These are five things about this animate world,
Which never can be known for certain, for no sign exists.

(a) There is no sign (*i.e.,* no clear indication) of the duration of life, because one cannot determine that so long will one live, and no longer. For beings may die in the first embryonic state, or in the second, third, or fourth, or after one month, or two, three, four, five or ten months, at the time when they issue from the womb, and further still at any time within or beyond one hundred years.

(b) There is also no sign of the (fatal) sickness, in so far as one cannot determine that beings will die of this or that sickness, and no other; for beings may die from a disease of the eyes, or the ears, or any other.

(c) There is also no sign of the time, in so far as one cannot determine that one will have to die just at this time of day and no other; for beings may die in the morning, or at midday, or at any other time.

(d) There is also no sign as to the laying down of the body; for, when one is dying, one cannot determine that the body should be laid down just here and not anywhere else. For the body of those born within a village may fall away outside the village; and those born outside a village may perish inside one; those born on land may perish in water, those born in water may perish on land; and so this might be expanded in various ways.

(e) There is also no sign of the future destiny, in so far as one cannot determine that one who has deceased there will be reborn here. For those who have deceased in the world of the Gods may be reborn among men, and those deceased in the world of men may be reborn in the world of the Gods, or anywhere else. In this way the world revolves round the five kinds of rebirth like an ox yoked to an oil-pressing mill.

7. *'Because the life-span is limited,'*—brief is the life of men at present; he lives long who lives for a hundred years, or a little more. Hence the Lord has said: 'Short, oh monks, is the life-span of men, transient, having its sequel elsewhere; one should do what is wholesome, one should lead a holy life, no one who is born can escape death; he lives long who lives for a hundred years, or a little more.

Short is the life of men, the good must scorn it,
And act as if their turban were ablaze.
For death is surely bound to come' (S I 108).

Furthermore, the whole Araka-Sutta (Anguttara IV 136–8) with its seven similies should be considered in detail: (*i.e.,* Life is fleeting, and passes away quickly, (a) like dewdrops on the tips of blades of grass which soon dry up when the sun rises; (b) or like the bubbles which rain causes in water, and which burst soon; (c) or like the line made by a stick in water, which vanishes soon; (d) or like a mountain brook, which does not stand still for a moment; (e) or like a gob of spittle spat out with ease; (f) or like a lump of meat thrown into a hot iron pot, which does not last long; (g) or like a cow about to be slaughtered; each time she raises her foot she comes nearer to death).

Furthermore He said: 'If, oh monks, a monk develops the recollection of death in such a way that he thinks,—"may I just live for one day and night,—for one day —, —for as long as it takes to eat an alms-meal,—for as long as it takes to chew and swallow four or five lumps of food,—and I will then attend to the Lord's religion, and much surely will still be done by me,"—then such monks are said to lead heedless lives, and they develop in a sluggish way the recollection of death which aims at the extinction of the outflows. But if, oh monks, a monk develops the recollection of death in such a way that he thinks,—"may I just live for so long as it takes to chew and swallow one lump of food,—were I to live just long enough to breathe in after breathing out, or to breathe out after breathing in,"—then such monks are said to lead watchful lives, and they develop keenly the recollection of death which aims at the extinction of the outflows' (A III 305–6). And the span of life is brief like a mere swallowing of four or five lumps of food, and it cannot be trusted.

8. *'From the shortness of the moment,'*—in ultimate reality beings live only for an exceedingly short moment, for it (life) lasts just as long as one single moment of thought. Just as a cart-wheel, whether it rolls along or stands still, always rests on one single spot of the rim; just so the life of beings lasts for one single moment of thought. As soon as that thought has ceased, the being also is said to have ceased. As it has been said: 'In the past thought-moment one has lived, but one does not live and one will not live in it; in the future thought-moment one has not lived, one does not live, but one will live; in

the present thought-moment one has not lived, but one does live, and one will not live in it.

Our life and our whole personality,
All our joys and all our pains,
Are bound up with one single thought,
And rapidly that moment passes.
And those skandhas which are stopped,
For one who's dying, or one remaining here,
They all alike have gone away,
And are no longer reproduced.
Nothing is born from what is unproduced;
One lives by that which is at present there.
When thought breaks up, then all the world is dead.
So't is when final truth the concept guides'

(Niddesa I 42).

(*Result*): When he recollects (death) from one or the other of these eight points of view, his mind by repeated attention becomes practised therein, mindfulness with death for its object is established, the hindrances are impeded, the Jhana-limbs become manifest. But because of the intrinsic nature of the object and the agitation it produces, the Jhana only reaches access and not full ecstasy.

(*Benefits*): And the monk who is devoted to this recollection of death is always watchful, he feels disgust for all forms of becoming, he forsakes the hankering after life, he disapproves of evil, he does not hoard up many things, and with regard to the necessities of life he is free from the taint of stinginess. He gains familiarity with the notion of impermanence, and, when he follows that up, also the notions of ill and not-self will stand out to him. At the hour of death, beings who have not developed the recollection of death, feel fear, fright and bewilderment, as if they were suddenly attacked by wild beasts, ghosts, snakes, robbers or murderers. He, on the contrary, dies without fear and bewilderment. If in this very life he does not win deathlessness, he is, on the dissolution of his body, bound for a happy destiny.

## 5. DISTASTE FOR THE BODY

### *a. The Thirty-two Parts of the Body*

(*The Formula*): *'And further, the disciple contemplates this body, from the sole of the foot upwards, and from the top of the head downwards, with a skin stretched over it, and filled with manifold impurities. There are in this body:*

*hairs of the head, hairs of the body, nails, teeth, skin;*
*muscles, sinews, bones, marrow, kidneys;*
*heart, liver, serous membranes, spleen, lungs;*
*intestines, mesentery, stomach, excrement, brain;*
*bile, digestive juices, pus, blood, grease, fat;*
*tears, sweat, spittle, snot, fluid of the joints, urine.'*

(*Buddhaghosa's comment*): From the sole of the feet upwards, from the top of the head downwards, in this carcass, bounded by the skin all round, and about six feet in length, although one may search everywhere, one does not see the least trace of anything that is actually pure, in the sense in which pearls, jewels, lapis lazuli, aloe wood, saffron, camphor, or aromatic powders are pure. But all one can see are manifold impurities, which consist of hairs of the head, hairs of the body, etc., and which are extremely malodorous, repulsive and unsightly.

(*The sevenfold method of learning*): 1. And here, when practising the attention to repulsiveness, even someone who knows the entire Tripitaka, should nevertheless, at the beginning of his work, first of all *verbally repeat* (the above formula). For to some people the mere repetition makes the subject of meditation manifest. This happened, for instance, to the two Elders who had a subject of meditation given to them by Mahādeva, the Elder who lived in Malaya. When asked for a subject of meditation, the Elder had given them the Pali text of the 32 parts of the body, requesting them to repeat just that for four months. And, although they were familiar with two or three Nikāyas, they repeated the thirty-two parts of the body for four months, and as a result of their correct method of learning they became streamwinners. And when reciting this formula one should arrange the items into groups of five (or six) (as shown above), and verbally repeat each group both forwards and backwards; *i.e.,* First: hairs of the head—skin; skin—hairs of the head. Then: muscles—kidneys; then: kidneys—hairs of the head. Then: heart—lungs; then: lungs—hairs of the head. And so on. In this way one should recite verbally a hundred times, a thousand times, or even a hundred thousand times. For by verbal repetition one becomes familiar with the text of the subject of meditation; and the mind does not run away here or there. The different constituents (of the body) become manifest, and stand out like a row of fingers, or of palings on a fence.

2. And one should *repeat* this not only verbally, but also *mentally.*

3. One should then determine the *colour* of the hairs. etc., as well as

4. their *shape.* Likewise

5. their *region,* the part above the navel being considered as the upper, the one below as the lower region. And likewise

6. the *locality* it occupies on the body. Finally,

7. its *delimitation*. There are two kinds of delimitation, by like parts and by unlike parts. 'This part of the body is limited by that other part below, above and round-about,'—that should be known as delimitation by like parts. 'Hairs of the head are not hairs of the body, and hairs of the body are not hairs of the head,'—that should be known as delimitation by unlike parts, in the sense that they are not mixed up (with one another).

(*Method of attending*): (This is tenfold; I give only the first five:) 1. One should attend *in regular order, i.e.,* from the time of recitation onwards one should attend to the parts of the body in their proper order, without passing any of them over. One should attend 2. *not too quickly,* nor 3. *too slowly.* 4. One should *ward off all distraction,* and 5. one must *transcend the notion* (of the parts of the body). This means: transcending the notions of 'hairs of the head, hairs of the body,' and so on, one should establish the mind in the idea of their repulsiveness. It is as if men, at a time when water is scarce, have found a well in the wood. They fix there some sort of a sign, such as a palm leaf, and with the help of that sign they manage to find their way back to bathe and to drink. But when by their repeated comings and goings the way has become obvious to them, then there is no more need for the sign, and they just go there at any time they like to bathe and drink. Even so, at the beginning, when one attends to the hairs of the head, hairs of the body, etc., as notions, it becomes obvious (in due course) that they are actually repulsive. Later on, however, one should go beyond the notions of the 'hairs of the head, hairs of the body,' etc., and establish the mind in just their repulsiveness.

(*Example*): First of all the disciple should take hold of

the mental image of the *hairs of the head*. And how? He should pull out one or two hairs from his head, place them on the palm of his hand, and first determine their *colour*. Or he may look at hairs in a place where hair has been cut, or he may look at the hairs which are found in a bowl of water or in a bowl full of rice-gruel. If they are black, he should attend to them as 'black,' if white as 'white,' but if they are mixed he should attend to the predominant colour.

When he has thus taken hold of the mental image, and determined all the parts of the body by way of colour, shape, region, locality and delimitation, he should determine the fivefold repulsiveness by way of colour, shape, smell, origin and locality.

The natural *colour* of the hairs of the head is black, like the berries of the soap tree. In shape they are long and round like the beam of a pair of scales. As to *region,* they grow in the upper region. As to their *locality,* they are bounded on both sides by the (roots of the) ears, in the front by the edge of the forehead, and at the back by the nape of the neck; the moist skin which covers the skull is the locality of the hairs of the head. As to their *delimitation,* the hairs of the head are limited on the inside by the surface of their own roots, which enter into the skin covering the skull as deep as the tip of a paddy blade, and by which they are fastened therein; on the outside by space; sideways by each other, because no two hairs are in one place. This is the delimitation by like parts. 'The hairs of the head are not hairs of the body, the hairs of the body are not the hairs of the head,'—in this way the hairs of the head are not mixed with the thirty-one parts of the body, for they form by themselves only one (separate) part: this is the delimitation by unlike parts.

And this is the determination of their *fivefold repulsiveness* by way of colour, etc.:

1. If people see in an inviting plate full of gruel or rice anything which looks like a hair, they become disgusted and say, 'that has hairs in it, take it away!' In this way hairs of the head are repulsive through their *colour* (or, their visual aspect).

2. When somebody eats at night, and feels (with his fingers) in his food the presence of vegetable fibres which have the shape of hairs, then he likewise becomes disgusted. In this way they are repulsive through their *shape*.

3. The *smell* of hairs which have not been oiled or perfumed is highly repulsive; and it is still more so when they are thrown on the fire. It is possible that hairs are occasionally none too repulsive by their colour or shape, but by their smell they are always repulsive. A baby's excrement may look in its colour like yellow turmeric, and in its shape it may be like a little heap of turmeric; or the swollen black corpse of a dog flung on to a rubbish heap may resemble in its colour a palm fruit, or in its shape a discarded round Mudinga drum, and its teeth may look like white jasmin buds: so both these things may occasionally be none too repulsive by their colour and shape, but by their smell they are sure to be repulsive.

4. Just as vegetables grown in an unclean place near where the village drains are discharged are repulsive and uneatable to towns' people, just so the hairs of the head are repulsive because they have grown as a result of the discharge of pus, blood, urine, excrement, bile, spittle, and so on. This is their repulsiveness from their *origin*.

5. And, like mushrooms which have arisen on a dung heap, these hairs of the head grow on the heap of the 31 parts. And because they grow in an unclean place, they are highly repugnant, like vegetables growing in burial grounds, or on rubbish heaps, or suchlike places, or the

red or blue water lilies which grow in ditches (into which many unclean things are thrown), and so on. This is their repulsiveness from their *locality*.

(And so for the other 31 parts.)

(*Result*): As a result, all the 32 parts of the body become manifest to him simultaneously, just as to a clear-sighted man, when he looks at a garland of 32 flowers of different hue strung on to one single thread, all these flowers become as it were manifest at once (simultaneously). . . . And when he turns his attention outside (to the bodies of other beings), then men, animals, etc., as they wander about, lose for him, when all these parts of the body have become manifest to him, the semblance of living beings and stand out to him merely as so many heaps of the parts. And the food, drink, etc., which they consume, appears as if thrown into these heaps of parts.

And the monk who is devoted to this mindfulness concerning that which belongs to the body 'conquers both delight and discontent; discontent does not conquer him; as soon as it arises, he overcomes it, and he dwells as one who has overcome it. Likewise he conquers fear and dread. He endures heat and cold . . . he becomes one who patiently endures even pains which threaten his life' (M iii 97).

### *b. The repulsiveness of food*

If someone wants to develop the notion of the repulsiveness of food, he should take up the subject of meditation, and, without missing even a single point of it, he should, in solitude and seclusion, contemplate the repulsiveness of the material food, which consists of things to eat, drink, chew and taste. And he should consider it from 10 points of view:

1. From having to *go* for it.—In order to get food, (by

begging, the monk) must go towards the village, like a jackal to a charnel field and, disregarding the delights of holy seclusion, he must leave behind him his religious retreat in the woods, free from the pressure of crowds, a place of happy solitude, offering water and shade, clean, cool and delightfully situated. (And on his way to the village he meets with many unpleasant sights and smells, he has to walk on uneven roads, full of stumps and thorns, and must watch out for dangers.)

2. From having to *seek* for it.—(When he walks along in the village, his feet sink deep into the mud, or, at other times, the wind covers him with dust, flies settle on him, etc. Some people give him no food, others stale or rotten food, others again are rude to him.)

3. From the *eating* of it.—Crushed (by the teeth) and smeared (with saliva) the chewed food becomes a mixture from which all visual beauty and good odour have disappeared, and it reaches a state of extreme repulsiveness, like dog's vomit in a dog's trough. And although it is in such a condition, one has to swallow it down, though at least it has passed out of the range of sight.

4. From the effect on the food of the *four effluvia*, *i.e.*, of bile, phlegm, pus and blood.

5. From the *receptacle,*—(*i.e.*, the stomach, which resembles a cesspool that has not been washed for a long time).

6. From its *undigested state.*—After it has reached this receptacle, the food, as long as it is undigested, remains in just that region, which is like an unwashed cesspool, pitch dark, traversed by winds which are scented with various rotten smells, excessively malodorous and loathsome. The food which has been swallowed to-day, yesterday, or the day before, becomes all one lump, enveloped in a membrane of phlegm, and it is digested by the body's heat, being covered in the process by the ac-

cumulated foam and bubbles to which the process of digestion gives rise. It has indeed become exceedingly loathsome.

7. From its *digested state*.—When it has been digested by the body's heat, the food is not transformed into something like gold or silver, as if it were gold-ore, silver-ore, and so on. But, constantly giving off foam and bubbles, it fills, having become excrement, the abdomen, —just as yellow loam, ground on a smooth grindstone, has been put into a tube; and, having become urine, it fills the bladder.

8. From its *effects*.—When well digested, the food brings forth the various putridities, such as the hairs of the head, hairs of the body, nails, teeth, etc. If not well digested, it produces hundreds of diseases, such as ringworm, itch, scab, leprosy, eczema, consumption, coughs, dysentery, etc.

9. From its *excretion*.—(a) When it is being swallowed, the food comes in by just one door, but when it is excreted it goes out through a number of them *i.e.* (as we read in the Suttanipāta 197 *sq.*), 'as eye-discharge from the eyes, as ear-wax from the ears' (and so on for the nine apertures). (b) At the time of swallowing one may consume it in great company, but when it comes to the excretion one expels just by oneself the food which has been transformed into excrement and urine. (c) At first, on the day when one consumes it, one is quite joyful, quite elated, full of zest and gladness; on the second day, when one expels it again, one holds one's nose, pulls a face, becomes disgusted and discontented. (d) At first, on the day when one swallows it down, one is full of passion and greed, fascinated and infatuated; the day after, when only one day has passed, one has lost all passion for it, and gets rid of it again, in a mood of incommodation, shame and loathing.

10. From the *soiling*.—(When it is being eaten, the food soils the hands, lips, tongue and palate. After it has been digested, it soils the tongue with saliva and phlegm, and the nine apertures with the substances which they discharge.)

(*Result*): In a monk who devotes himself to the notion of the repulsiveness of food, the mind withdraws from the greed for tastes, keeps away from it, turns away from it. Just to avoid suffering he takes food, without becoming intoxicated by it, even as a traveller, in his desire to get out of a desert, may eat the flesh of his own child. And then, without much further trouble, the disciple learns, as a result of his comprehension of the nature of material food, to look through the greed for the five sense-qualities. And this again leads to a fuller understanding of the skandha of form. He perfects the development of his mindfulness as regards the body (see II 5a) by means of (his insight into) the repulsiveness of undigested food, and so on, and he progresses on the road which will facilitate his further advance to the 'perception of the Foul' (see II 5c).

### *c. The Foul. The Corpses on the charnel field*

'And further, if the disciple, sees (1) a corpse, thrown on the charnel field, dead for one, two or three days, swollen, blueish and festering, he draws along his own body for comparison, and thinks: "Verily, also this body of mine is subject to such a law, is going to be like that, and it has not gone beyond this."

And he thinks the same when he sees (2) a corpse eaten by crows, hawks, vultures, dogs, jackals, or many kinds of worms; (3) a chain of bones (skeleton), with some flesh and blood remaining, and held together by the tendons; (4) a chain of bones, without flesh, but smeared with blood, held together through the tendons; (5) a chain of bones from which both flesh and blood have departed, but still held together through the tendons; (6) bones unconnected, scattered in all directions, —here a bone of the hand, and there a bone of the foot, a shin bone, a thigh bone, the pelvis, a vertebral bone, the skull; (7) bones white, similar in colour to shells; (8) bones, more than a year old, made into a heap; (9) bones which have gone rotten and have become dust.'

So far the Satipatthānasutta. In the Visuddhimagga (chapter VI 1 *sq.*) the subject is arranged as the tenfold Foulness of corpses, *i.e.*, 1. the swollen corpse; 2. the blueish corpse; 3. the festering corpse, which exudes pus; 4. the fissured corpse; 5. the corpse gnawed and mangled by dogs, jackals, and so on; 6. the corpse of which the various parts are scattered about; 7. the corpse which is both hacked and scattered; 8. the corpse which is smeared with the blood which drips from it; 9. the corpse infested with worms; 10. the bones, either the whole skeleton, or single bones.

And (1) the swollen corpse, as demonstrating the downfall of the shape of the body, is beneficial for one who lusts after beautiful shapes. (2) The blueish corpse, as demonstrating the ruin of the colour of the skin, is beneficial for one who lusts after the beauty of the skin. (3) The festering corpse, as demonstrating the bad stench which is bound up with the sores of the body, is beneficial for one who lusts after the odours of the body that are produced by flowers, perfumes, and so on. (4) The fissured corpse, as demonstrating that the body is hollow within, is beneficial for one who lusts after solidity and fulness in the body. (5) The gnawed corpse, as demonstrating the destruction of the once proud outlines of the protrusions of the flesh, is beneficial for one who lusts after the protrusions of the flesh, at the breasts or in similar parts of the body. (6) The scattered corpse, as demonstrating the dismemberment of the limbs, large and small, is beneficial for one who lusts after the graceful combination of the limbs. (7) The hacked and scattered corpse, as demonstrating how the build of the body can be broken up and contorted, is beneficial for one who lusts after perfection in the build of the body. (8) The bloody corpse, by demonstrating the repulsiveness of a body smeared with blood, is beneficial for one who lusts after the beauty produced by adornment. (9) The worm-eaten corpse, by demonstrating that the body belongs in common to manifold kinds of worms (see II 4), is beneficial for one who lusts after his body with the thought, 'this is mine.' (10) The skeleton, as demonstrating the repulsive state of the bones of the body, is beneficial for one who lusts after the perfection of the teeth. In this way, the Foul should be understood as tenfold by way of its relation to the different kinds of lustful behaviour.

And although this object is repulsive, zest and gladness nevertheless arise in the disciple, partly because he sees the advantages of it, and thinks, 'surely by such progress I shall be freed from old age and death,' and partly because he forsakes the torments which the hindrances bring with them. He is like a dustman who rejoices at the sight of a rubbish heap, since he sees therein an advantage to himself, and thinks, 'Now I shall get so much in wages'; or he is like a sick man, who suffers from the pains of sickness, (and who rejoices at their alleviation) through the application of emetics and purgatives.

Although it is tenfold, the Foul has just one single mark. All these ten objects have for their mark the fact that they are unclean, evil-smelling, loathsome and repulsive. And it appears with this mark not only in a dead body, but also in a living body, as with the Elder Mahātissa of Mount Cetiya when he saw the teeth(-bones of a laughing woman; see p. 80). For just like the dead body, so also the living one is an abomination. And since it is concealed by adventitious adornments, this mark of abominableness is not clearly perceived.

But by its nature this body is an accumulation of more than 300 bones, joined together by 180 joints, held together by 900 tendons, bedaubed with 900 pieces of flesh, enveloped in a moist outer skin, covered with an inner skin, full of gaps and holes, with something oozing and trickling out all the time, as if it were a saucepan for frying fat; frequented by hosts of worms, a field for diseases, a basis for painful states; like a long-standing boil which has burst open, it constantly discharges impurities from the nine apertures, which are like so many wounds: filth oozes from the two eyes, and from the two ears, snot from the nostrils, food, bile, phlegm and blood from the mouth, excrement and urine from the lower apertures; from the 99,000 pores an impure sweaty fluid oozes out and causes bluebottle flies and so on to gather round. Unless one takes care of it,—by the use of tooth-picks, by washing the face, oiling the hair, bathing the body, clothing it, and dressing it up,—even a king, if he were to wander from village to village in a state of nature, with his hair all rough and dishevelled, would be undistinguishable from any rubbish-remover or outcast, because the body would be equally repulsive in either case. Therefore, as regards its unclean, evil-smelling loathsome and repulsive condition, there is no difference between the body of a king and that of an outcast. When, with the help of tooth-picks, by washing the face, and so on, one has removed the dirt from the teeth, and so on, when one has covered up the private parts with various garments, when one has anointed the body with sweet-smelling ointments of the most various colours, when one has adorned it with flowers, ornaments, and suchlike, then one manages to give it an appearance which makes it possible to seize upon it as 'I and mine.' Hence it is because they do not perceive the mark of abominableness, which characterizes the true and proper nature of the body, but which is concealed from them by the adventitious adornments, that men take delight in women, and women in men. But in reality there is in the body not even the tiniest spot that would be worth regarding as delightful.

## 6. THE GOAL (NIRVANA)

### THE RECOLLECTION OF PEACE

(*The formula*): If someone wants to develop the Recollection of Peace he should, in solitude and seclusion, recall the qualities of Nirvana, which is defined as the appeasing of all ill, with the words: *'As far as there are dharmas, conditioned or unconditioned, dispassion has been taught as the highest of these dharmas, i.e., the sobering down of self-intoxication, the removal of thirst, the uprooting of clinging, the halting of the round (of Samsara), the extinction of craving, dispassion, stopping, Nirvana'* (A ii 34).

(*Explanation*): *'Dharmas'* are (things considered in) their own-being (as they really are). *'Conditioned or unconditioned,'*—made, or not made, by the combination and concurrence of conditions. And here *dispassion* does not only mean the bare absence of greed; but it should be taken as that unconditioned Dharma which gets the epithets of (the above statement), *i.e.*, the sobering down of self-intoxication, etc., up to: Nirvana.

And because thanks to it all forms of intoxication, like self-conceit, intoxication with one's manhood, etc., are sobered down, are disintoxicated and destroyed, therefore one speaks of *'the sobering down of self-intoxication.'* And because thanks to it also all sensuous thirst is removed, disappears, therefore it is called *'the removal of thirst.'* And because thanks to it the clingings to the five sense-qualities are uprooted, therefore it is called *'the uprooting of clinging.'* And because thanks to it the round (of samsaric life) in the triple world is halted, therefore it is called the *'halting of the round (of Samsara).'* And because thanks to it craving is in every way extinguished, fades away, and is stopped, therefore it is called *'the extinction of craving, dispassion, stopping.'* And it is called *Nirvana* because it has left craving behind, has escaped from it, is dissociated from that craving which goes by the name of 'weaving' (*vāna*), on account of the fact that it ties, binds, stitches into an ever repeated series of existences the four forms of life, the five places of rebirth, the seven stations of conscious life and the nine abodes of sentient beings.

(*Other epithets of Nirvana*): In this way one should call to mind Peace which is defined as Nirvana by way of its qualities, such as the 'sobering down of intoxication,' etc. In addition one should also recall the qualities of Peace as they are taught by the Lord in other Sutras, as for instance (S iv 360–72): 'The Unconditioned, oh monks, I will point out to you, the Truth, the Other Shore, That which is hard to see, the Ageless, the Everlasting, That which is beyond all multiplicity, the Deathless, the Bliss, Safety, the Wonderful, the Undistressed, the Trouble-free, Purity, the Island, the Shelter, the Place of Rest,' and so on.

(*Limitations*): Like all the six recollections, so also this one can be properly and successfully accomplished only on the level of sainthood (*i.e.*, after one has entered the First Path). Nevertheless also the worlding should attend to it, if he attaches weight to Peace. For even if one only hears of it, the mind brightens up at the thought of Peace.

(*Results*): And the monk who is devoted to the recollection of Peace sleeps at ease, wakes up at ease, is calm in his faculties, calm in his mind, endowed with a sense of shame and a dread of blame, amiable, intent on sublime things, respected and honoured by his brethren. Even if he do not penetrate any further, he is at least bound for a happy destiny.

# III

## TRANCE

### I. THE PRACTICE OF INTROVERSION

#### *a. Withdrawal from the world*

1. With his vigour grown strong, his mind should be placed in samadhi;
For if thought be distracted we lie in the fangs of the passions.

2. No distractions can touch the man who's alone both in his body and mind.
Therefore renounce you the world, give up all thinking discursive!

3. Thirsting for gain, and loving the world, the people fail to renounce it.
But the wise can discard this love, reflecting as follows:

4. Through stillness joined to insight true,
His passions are annihilated.
Stillness must first of all be found.
That springs from disregarding worldly satisfactions.

5. Shortlived yourself, how can you find that others, quite as fleeting, are worthy of your love?
Thousands of births will pass without a sight of him you cherish so.

6. When unable to see your beloved, discontent disturbs your samadhi;
When you have seen, your longing, unsated as ever, returns as before.

7. Then you forfeit the truth of the Real; your fallen condition shocks you no longer;
Burning with grief you yearn for re-union with him whom you cherish.

8. Worries like these consume a brief life,—over and over again to no purpose;
You stray from the Dharma eternal, for the sake of a transient friend.

9. To share in the life of the foolish will lead to the states of woe;
You share not, and they will hate you; what good comes from contact with fools?

10. Good friends at one time, of a sudden they dislike you,
You try to please them, quite in vain,—the worldly are not easily contented!

11. Advice on their duties stirs anger; your own good deeds they impede;
When you ignore what they say they are angry, and head for a state of woe.

12. Of his betters he is envious, with his equals there is strife;
To inferiors he is haughty, mad for praise and wroth of blame;
Is there ever any goodness in these foolish common men?

13. Self-applause, belittling others, or encouragement to sin,
Some such evil's sure to happen where one fool another meets.

14. Two evils meet when fools consort together.
Alone I'll live, in peace and with unblemished mind.

15. Far should one flee from fools. When met, they should be won by kindness,
Not in the hope of intimacy, but so as to preserve an even, holy, mind.

16. Enough for Dharma's work I'll take from him, just as a bee takes honey from a flower.
Hidden and unknown, like the new moon, I will live my life.

24. The fools are no one's friends, so have the Buddhas taught us;
They cannot love unless their interest in themselves impels them.

26. Trees do not show disdain, and they demand no toilsome wooing;
Fain would I now consort with them as my companions.

27. Fain would I dwell in a deserted sanctuary, beneath a tree, or in a cave,
In noble disregard for all, and never looking back on what I left.

28. Fain would I dwell in spacious regions owned by no one,

And there, a homeless wanderer, follow my own mind,

29. A clay bowl as my only wealth, a robe that does not tempt the robbers,
Dwelling exempt from fear, and careless of my body.

33. Alone a man is born, and quite alone he also meets his death;
This private anguish no one shares; and friends can only bar true welfare.

34. Those who travel through Becoming should regard each incarnation
As no more than a passing station on their journey through Samsara.

38. So will I ever tend delightful and untroubled solitude,
Bestowing bliss, and stilling all distractions.

39. And from all other cares released, the mind set on collecting my own spirit,
To unify and discipline my spirit I will strive.

### *b. The eight stages of trance*

*The first stage:*
*'Detached from sense-desires, detached (also from the other four) unwholesome states, he dwells in the attainment of the first jhāna, which is accompanied by applied and discursive thinking, born of detachment, rapturous and joyful.'*

*Rapturous and joyful:* 'Rapture' is here bound up with surgency. It has the property of being pleased; it consists in a swelling up of body and mind, or it pervades body and mind with a thrill; it manifests itself by exaltation. Rapture is of five kinds: Slight rapture, momentary rapture, overflowing rapture, transporting rapture, all-pervading rapture. Among these (1) the slight rapture is just able to make the hairs of the body stand on end. (2) The momentary rapture is like the (repeated) production of lightning from moment to moment. (3) Just as waves overflow the shore and then break, so the overflowing rapture repeatedly floods the body and then breaks. (4) The transporting rapture is powerful, and can lift up the body, to the extent of causing actual levitation. (5) Finally, when all-pervading rapture takes place, the entire body is completely surcharged with it, like a fully blown-up bladder, or like a mountain cavern suddenly filled with a mighty flood of water.

And as this fivefold rapture becomes pregnant and matures, it brings about the two kinds of tranquillity, the tranquillity of mental activities (*i.e.*, of feelings, perceptions and impulses) and the tranquillity of consciousness (itself). As tranquillity becomes pregnant and matures, it brings about the two kinds of joy, joy of body and joy of mind. As joy becomes pregnant and matures, it brings about the threefold concentration,—momentary concentration, access concentration and ecstatic concentration. And among the five kinds of rapture the all-pervading rapture is meant here. As the root of ecstatic concentration it keeps on growing until it unites with the samādhi.

Now as to the other term, 'joy.' It has the property of feeling well; it leads to the expansion of the mental states associated with it, and it manifests itself by helping them along. Although rapture and joy are often found together, they nevertheless differ in that rapture is the satisfaction from obtaining the desired object, whereas joy is the enjoyment of that which has been obtained. Wherever there is rapture, there is joy also. But where there is joy, there is not necessarily rapture also (as for instance in the third jhana). Rapture is grouped with the skandha of impulses, joy with the skandha of feeling. Like some weary man in a desert, who sees a wood or water, or hears of them,—so is rapture; like his enjoyment when he enters into the shade of the wood or when he drinks the water,—that is joy.

*Endowment with five factors:* Applied thinking first implants the mind in the object; discursive thinking keeps it continually engaged on it; in the mind which with their help strives to accomplish non-distraction the rapture, which has been made possible by the success of the striving, causes an upsurge, and the joy and expansion. Assisted by this implanting, sustained attention, upsurge and expansion, one-pointedness places the mind, with the remaining associated states (*e.g.*, contact), evenly and well on one single object. The 'endowment with the five factors' should therefore be understood as the arising of these five, *i.e.*, of applied thinking, discursive thinking, rapture, joy and one-pointedness of thought. For when these five have arisen, so has the trance. Hence they are called its five endowing factors.

*Conditions of continued success:* But if the monk has not thoroughly impeded his sense-desires by the contemplation of the dangers of sense-objects (see p. 85), and so on (see pp. 73–4), if he has not thoroughly tranquillized his inner depravities through winning the tranquillity of his mental activities; if he has not thoroughly driven out all sloth and torpor, by mentally getting to work on the task of rousing his energies, and so on; if he has not thoroughly uprooted his excitedness and sense of guilt by mentally getting to work on the signs of calm, and so on; if he has not thoroughly removed the other obstacles to concentration (such as indecision),—and if nevertheless he enters into trance, then he will quickly come out of it again, like a bee that has entered its uncleaned hive, or like a king who has gone into an untidy garden. But when he enters into trance after he has thoroughly removed the obstacles to concentration, then he can remain all day long in its attainment, just as a bee that has entered its well-cleaned hive, or as a king who has gone into a well-tidied garden.

*The second stage:*

*'From the appeasing of applied and discursive thinking, he dwells in the attainment of the second jhana, where the inward heart is serene and uniquely exalted, and which is devoid of applied and discursive thinking, born of concentration, rapturous and joyful.'*

*Inward* is here to be understood as 'one's own inwardness,' and it means 'born in oneself,' 'produced in one's own continuity.'

*Serene:* This refers to faith. As joined to faith the trance is deemed to be serene, just as a cloth steeped in a blue dye is deemed to be blue. Or, this trance is called 'serene' because it makes the heart serene, partly because it is accompanied by faith, and partly because it appeases the disturbing applied and discursive thinking.

*Uniquely exalted* (*ekodibhāva*): 'Alone by itself (*eko*) it rises up (*udeti*),' therefore is it called *ekodi*. The meaning is that, no longer overgrown with applied and discursive thinking, it can now rise up as the highest and best. For it is quite usual to call the best 'unique.' Or one may explain the term as meaning that 'being free from applied and discursive thinking, it is alone, without companion.' Alternatively, *udi* may mean that it raises, or causes to arise, the mental states associated (with this trance).

That first jhana, because disturbed by applied and discursive thinking, is not quite serene, just as water is not quite clear when confused by waves large and small. In spite of the fact that faith is present in it, it is therefore not called 'serene.' And because that first trance is not quite serene, the concentration is also not fully manifested therein, and that is why the state of unique exaltation has not been predicated of it. But in this jhana the obstacles of applied and discursive thinking are absent, and in consequence faith has an opportunity to unfold itself and becomes quite powerful; and the concentration is more fully manifested, because it has gained that strong faith for its ally.

*Born of concentration:* means either that it is born of the concentration of the first jhana, or that it is born of the concentration associated (with the state of mind prevalent in the second jhana). Also the first jhana is born of the concentration associated (with it), but in fact only this second jhana deserves to be properly called 'concentration': from the absence of the disturbing applied and discursive thinking it becomes quite unshakable and most serene. Therefore, in order to praise it, just this trance is called 'born of concentration.'

*The third stage:*
*'Through distaste for rapture, he dwells evenmindedly, mindful and clearly conscious; he experiences with this body that joy of which the Ariyans declare, "joyful lives he who is evenminded and mindful." It is thus that he dwells in the attainment of the third jhana.'*

*The fourth stage:*
*'From the forsaking of joy, from the forsaking of pain, from the going to rest of his former gladness and sadness, he dwells in the attainment of the fourth jhana, which is neither painful nor pleasurable,—in utter purity of even-mindedness and mindfulness.'*

*The fifth stage:*
*'By passing quite beyond all perceptions of form, by the going to rest of the perceptions of impact, by not attending to the perception of manifoldness, on thinking "Endless Space," he dwells in the attainment of the station of endless space.'*

*The sixth stage:*
*'By passing quite beyond the station of endless space, on thinking "endless consciousness," he dwells in the attainment of the station of unlimited consciousness.'*

*The seventh stage:*
*'By passing quite beyond the station of unlimited consciousness, on thinking "There is not anything," he dwells in the attainment of the station of nothing whatever.'*

*The eighth stage:*
*'By passing quite beyond the field of nothing whatever, he dwells in the attainment of the station of neither perception nor non-perception.'*

## 2. THE CULTIVATION OF THE SOCIAL EMOTIONS

### *a. Nine preliminary reflections on hate*

1. The disciple admonishes himself in the following way: 'Shame on you, you furious man!' (a) Has not the Lord

said: 'Even if, oh monks, robbers or government agents would, with a double-handed saw, cut a man limb from limb, if his mind would be filled with hostility thereat, he would on that account not be a follower of my religion' (M i 129). (b) Moreover (S i 162):

> 'Of these the worse is he who to one angry
> Replies with wrath.
> Do not reply with wrath to one who's angry
> And win a battle hard to win!
> You course then for the weal of both,
> Yourself and of the other one.
> You understand the other's angry mood,
> Remaining mindful and at peace.'

(c) Moreover (A iv 94–6): 'These seven things, oh monks, pleasing to an enemy, caused by an enemy, befall those who are angry, be they man or woman. And which seven? Here, oh monks, an enemy wishes that his enemy might be ugly. And why? Because an enemy takes no pleasure in an enemy's beauty. But the man who is angry, overcome by anger, under the sway of anger, although he may be well washed, well anointed, neat in his hair and beard, and clad all in spotless white; yet for all that he is ugly to look at when overcome by anger. And so with the other things which an enemy wishes to an enemy, *i.e.*, that he should sleep badly; be without the good things of life; without wealth; without reputation; without friends. Finally, an enemy wishes that his enemy should not, when his body breaks up, after death, be reborn with a happy destiny, in the heavenly world. And why? Because an enemy takes no pleasure in the idea of an enemy's going to a happy destiny. The man who is angry, overcome by anger, under the sway of anger, misconducts himself in deed, word and thought, and in consequence, when his body breaks up, after death, overcome by anger, he will be reborn in a place of woe, with an evil destiny, in a state of punishment, in the hells.'

2. If by this kind of striving and struggling the aversion is appeased, well and good. If not, he should dispel his malice by recalling some peace-bringing and pure property in his foe. When recalled it will bring serenity. (And there are here five possibilities:) (a) Some people are calm in their bodily behaviour, and everyone notices the calm they display in the discharge of their many duties. But their behaviour in speech and in mind is not calm. This side of their behaviour should be disregarded, and only the calm of their bodily behaviour recalled. (b) Others are calm in their behaviour when speaking, and this their calm is noticed by all, for by nature they are skilled in welcoming people politely, friendly in their speech, agreeable conversationalists, sympathetic, their speech easy to understand and obliging, and they propound the Dharma in sweet tones, and preach sermons about the Dharma in well-rounded sentences and expressions. But their behaviour in body and in mind is not calm. This side of their behaviour one should disregard, and recall only the calm of their behaviour when speaking. (c) Others are calm in their mental behaviour, and the calm they display when saluting a shrine, and in similar actions, is noticed by all. For someone who is not calm in his mind, when saluting a shrine, or the Bodhi-tree, or the Elders, does so without respectful care; or in the hall where he listens to the Dharma he sits with his mind disturbed, or (sleepily) flutters with his eye-lids. But someone who is calm in his mind salutes with trusting confidence and respectful care; he listens to the Dharma with his ears open and appreciates its value; and his mental serenity shines through in his body and speech. In this sense someone's mental behaviour only is calm, but his behaviour with body and speech may not be calm. Disregarding this side of their

behaviour, one should recall only the calm of their mental behaviour. (d) In the case of other people again, not one even of these three things is calm. Towards such persons one should nurse compassion, and think, 'although at present he still lives in the world of men, soon, when only a few days have passed, he will find himself in the eight great hells and the sixteen Ussada hells.' For through compassion malice is appeased. (e) In the case of others again all three things are calm. One may then think of him as he behaves with his body, or when he speaks, or of his mind,—just as one likes. For the development of friendliness for such a person is not difficult.

3. If in spite of these endeavours the malice still continues to rise up, the disciple should admonish himself as follows: 'If your enemy has done some harm to you within the sphere of what you regard as your own, why do you want to inflict further harm on your own mind, which lies outside his sphere (of influence)? You have left your kith and kin, ever ready to help you, their tears streaming down; why can you not also leave this wrath, a foe who brings you a great deal of misfortune? You cherish this wrath, which nevertheless cuts off by the root those very (moral) precepts which you try to keep; is there a fool like you? You are angry because someone has done you a low deed; why then do you want yourself to do a deed of the same kind? If, in his desire to make you furious, someone is unpleasant to you, why then do you fulfil his wishes by rising up in fury? Whether in your anger you inflict harm on him or not, in any case you torment yourself with the pain that comes from wrath. If foes, blinded by wrath, tread the unprofitable path (of hatred), why then, by becoming angry, do you follow their example? That hatred which induced your enemy to do to you what you did not like, —just that hatred you should cut off; what are you

groundlessly vexed with? There is the momentariness of dharmas, and the skandhas with which he has been unpleasant to you have ceased to be: with what then are you angry that is here and now? If someone does harm to someone else, who does he harm to, except himself? You yourself are the root cause of your ills. What therefore are you angry with him for?'

4. If, in spite of the fact that he has admonished himself in this way, his aversion is not appeased, he should contemplate the fact that both he and the other are the products of their own deeds (see p. 75). And he should at first contemplate this fact with regard to himself, as follows: 'Now listen, what will you in your anger do to him? Will not this deed of yours, which has originated in hate, be conducive to your misfortune? For you are the owner of your deeds, the heir of your deeds, your deeds are the source of what you are, they are your close kinsmen, they are your refuge (protection). You will be the heir of whatever deed you may do. But this deed of yours will not enable you to achieve the full enlightenment of a Buddha, or the enlightenment of a Pratyekabuddha, or the level of a Disciple, or some happy destiny, such as that of Brahmā, Śakra, a universal monarch, a local king, and so on; but it will make you fall away from the holy religion, and lead you into an existence where you will feed on scraps, and suffer the exquisite torments of the hells, etc. When you act like this, you are like a man who, having seized glowing coals or dung with both his hands, wants to hit someone else with them, but first of all he burns and befouls himself.' And the same reflections should be applied to the other person. . . . He is like a man who, facing the wind, wants to throw dust on to somebody else, though he only throws it on himself.

5. If in spite of these reflections his hatred is not ap-

peased, he should contemplate the virtues of the Teacher's conduct in the past (see pp. 52–6).

6. If, because he has been for such a long time a slave of the defiling passions, even as a result of his contemplating the Teacher's conduct in the past this his aversion is not appeased, he then should contemplate what is said about the samsaric world which is without beginning and end, *i.e.*, 'It is not easy, monks, to find a being who has not in the past been one's mother, or one's father, brother, sister, son or daughter' (S ii 189–90). Therefore one should raise with regard to that person a thought as follows: 'This then has been in the past my mother, who sheltered me for ten months in her belly, who removed my urine, excrement, spittle, snot, etc., without loathing, as if it had been golden sandalwood, allowed me to dance on her breast, carried me on her hips, and brought me up. When he was my father he braved goat tracks and rough roads to pursue his trade; for my sake he sacrificed his life, he went into battle with both armies drawn up against each other, by ship he took to the great ocean, and he did other difficult deeds; in order to be able to bring up his children he acquired wealth by these various devices, and so he brought me up. And when he was my brother, sister, son or daughter, he did me this or that service. It is therefore not suitable that my mind should feel hate for him.'

7. If the disciple is still unable to pacify his heart, he should contemplate the advantages of friendliness: Listen, my recluse, has not the Lord said, 'Monks, when friendliness, liberating the heart, has been cultivated, developed, been made much of, been made into a vehicle of progress, and a foundation of life, been confirmed again and again, mastered and well brought to perfection, eleven advantages can be expected. Which eleven? 1. At ease he sleeps, 2. at ease he wakes up, 3. he

sees no bad dreams, 4. he is dear to men, 5. he is dear to ghosts, 6. deities guard him, 7. fire, poison and sword cannot affect him; 8. quickly he concentrates his mind; 9. his features are serene, and 10. he dies unbewildered. 11. Even though he may not penetrate any further, he is one who goes up to Brahma's world' (A v 342)? If you do not extinguish in you this thought of hate, you will be excluded from these advantages.

1. *At ease he sleeps, i.e.,* he does not sleep badly as other people do who roll over from side to side, and snore loudly. When he falls asleep he is like one who has entered on the attainment of trance. 2. *At ease he wakes up, i.e.,* he does not wake up badly as people do who, on waking up, moan, yawn and roll over from side to side. At ease, steadily, he wakes, like a lotus flower which opens up. 3. *He sees no bad dreams, i.e.,* even though he may dream, he has auspicious dreams, dreaming that he salutes a shrine, or performs an act of worship, or listens to the Dharma. But he has no bad dreams like other people who dream that they are surrounded by robbers, attacked by wild beasts, or precipitated down a steep cliff. 4. *He is dear to men:* he is dear and agreeable to men like a string of pearls which adorns the breast, or like a wreath of flowers worn on the head. 5. *He is dear to ghosts:* as he is dear to men, so also to non-human beings. 6. *Deities guard him:* as parents guard their son. 7. *Fire, poison, and sword cannot affect him, i.e.,* they cannot affect, cannot enter, cannot upset his body. So it is said. 8. *Quickly he concentrates his mind,* and he is free from dull stupefaction. 9. *His features are serene:* like a ripe palm fruit which has just fallen from the stalk. 10. *He dies unbewildered:* for one who dwells in friendliness there is no such thing as a death in bewildered confusion. But unbewildered he dies, as though falling asleep. 11. *Even though he may not penetrate any*

*further:* if he is not able to proceed, beyond the attainment of friendliness, to Arhatship, he will be reborn, on having deceased here, in the world of Brahmā, like one who has awoken from his sleep.

8. If even in this way he cannot extinguish his hate, he should undertake the analysis of the elements. And how? 'Listen, you recluse, when you are angry with him, what are you angry with? Are you angry with the hairs of the head, or the hairs of the body, or the nails, or any of the other 32 parts of the body? Or are you perhaps angry with the element of earth, water, fire, air, in the hairs of the head, etc.? Or, as concerns the 5 skandhas, the 12 sense-fields, and the 18 elements, thanks to which this person is called by this or that name,—among them are you angry with the skandha of form, or that of feeling, perception, impulses or consciousness? Or are you angry with the sense-field of the eye, or of sight-objects, etc.? Or are you angry with the element of the eye, or the element of sight-objects, or the element of eye-consciousness, etc., etc.?' When he carries out this kind of analysis of the elements, there is no place where the wrath can find a footing, no more than there is for a mustard seed on the point of an awl, or for a painting in the empty sky.

9. But if he is not able to perform the analysis of the elements, he should perform an exchange of gifts. Of his own belongings he should give to the other, and he should receive from the other something that belongs to him. But if the other is without means, or has (as a monk) no right to dispose of his property, he should just give of his own. If he does so, the malice of that person will certainly be appeased.

(*1. Preliminaries*): The Yogin, who is a beginner and who wants, among the four stations of Brahma, first of all to develop friendliness, should remove the outer obstacles (see VM ch. IV), receive the subject of meditation, finish his meal, dispel the drowsiness following on it, and sit at his ease in a secluded spot on a well-arranged seat. He should then, to begin with, contemplate the dangers of hate and the advantages of forbearance. And why? For through this meditational development hatred ought to be forsaken, forbearance ought to be reached. But it is not possible to forsake something without having seen its dangers, nor to reach something without having understood its advantages. Therefore the dangers of hatred should be seen by means of such Suttas as: 'Friend, full of hatred, overcome by hatred, with their minds overpowered by hatred, people take life' (A i 216 and 189). And the advantages of forbearance should be understood by such passages as:

'Patience and forbearance is the highest penance.
The Buddhas call it the highest Nirvana' (Dhp. 184).
'Strong in patience, armed with its strength,—
Him I call a Brahmin' (Dhp. 399).
'There is nothing better than patience' (S i 222).

Therefore the disciple should undertake the development of friendliness, so as to separate his mind from the hate, of which he has seen the dangers, and to conjoin it with patience, of which he has understood the advantages.

(*2. The four persons. 2a. Unsuitable persons*): He should from the start know about the persons who are unsuitable, *i.e.,* friendliness should either not be developed towards them in the beginning, or it should not be developed towards them at all. For in the beginning this friendliness should not be developed for these four, *i.e.*, undear persons, excessively dear friends, indifferent people, hostile persons. It should not be developed at all for a definite person of the opposite sex, and also not for the dead. To try and treat an undear person as dear is tiresome; and likewise it is hard to treat an excessively dear friend as an indifferent person, since we are inclined to weep if even the least evil happens to him; and an indifferent person cannot easily be treated as either important or dear. When one thinks of a foe, wrath is apt to arise. Lust arises when friendliness is directed on a definite person of the opposite sex. And when developed for the dead, neither access nor ecstasy can be reached.

(*2b. Suitable object*): First of all friendliness should again and again be developed for *oneself*, 'May I be happy, free from ill,' or, 'May I be free from enmity, free from injury, free from disturbance, and may I preserve myself at ease!'

(*2c. Extension to others*): Developing the wish, 'May I be well,' and taking himself as a witness, the disciple produces then the wish that other beings also should have well-being and ease, *i.e.*, 'As I want to be happy, am averse to suffering, want to live and do not want to die, so also other beings.' In order that he may take himself as a witness, he must therefore first of all radiate friendliness on to himself. Immediately after that, so that he may proceed easily, he should think of his *dear*, pleasant, respected teacher or preceptor, or of someone who is like him, as well as of his generosity, his friendly words, etc., which make him so dear and pleasant, and of his moral virtue, learning, etc., which make him so respected. And the disciple should develop friendliness for him, in this manner: 'May this good man be free from ill,' and so on. And for a person of this kind fully concentrated friendliness is accomplished whenever one wishes. But the monk who is not content with just that, and who wants to abolish the barriers (between himself, dear, indifferent and hostile persons), should immediately after that develop friendliness for 2. a *very dear person,* then 3. for an *indifferent person,* 4. then for an *enemy.* While he meditates thus, he should, as soon as he has made the mind soft and pliant in one compartment, direct it on to the next one. If, while he directs his mind on to the enemy, aversion arises in him on remembering the offences that enemy has committed, he should again and again accomplish an attitude of friendliness towards the first three kinds of person. Then, emerging from that, he should dispel the aversion by again and again feeling friendly towards that last person (*i.e.,* the enemy). When he has appeased his aversion for the hostile person, his mind proceeds in friendliness also towards him, just as it does to dear persons, very dear friends and indifferent persons.

(*3. Friendliness becomes unlimited. 3a. The task*): Then, as he feels friendliness again and again, he should achieve an even mind towards the four persons,—*i.e.,* himself, a dear person, an indifferent person, a foe,—and bring about the abolition of the barriers between them.

(*3b. The token*): And this is here the token (of his success): Suppose this person were seated in a certain place together with a dear, indifferent, and hostile person,—he himself being the fourth. Robbers would come along, and say: 'Venerable ones, give us one of the monks!' To the question, 'what for?', they would answer: 'so as to kill him, to take the blood from his throat, and offer it in sacrifice.' Now if that monk should think, 'let them take this one or that one,' he has not accomplished the breakdown of the boundaries. And if he thinks, 'let them take me, and not those three,' he has also not accomplished it. And why not? Because he does not seek the benefit of him whose capture he desires, but that of the others only. But when he sees none among the four whom he would hand over to the robbers, then his mind proceeds just evenly towards himself and the other three, and he has broken down the barriers.

(*3c. The level of trance*): Immediately together with the breaking down of the barriers, the monk has acquired the mental image and access concentration. But when he has broken down the barriers, and then tends, develops and cultivates that mental image, he attains full concentration without much trouble,—and that successively on the four stages of Jhāna.

(*3d. The canonical formula*): For by means of one or the other of these four levels of jhāna 'he dwells suffusing first one direction with a heart linked to friendliness, then a second, then a third, then a fourth, then above, below, around, and everywhere. And so he dwells, recognizing himself in all, suffusing the entire world with a heart linked to friendliness, far-reaching, gone great, unlimited, free from enmity and malice.' This miraculous transformation can be achieved only by persons whose thought has reached full concentration through one of the four jhānas.

Here: *suffusing* means: he touches, makes into an object. *Recognizing himself in all* (*sabbattatāya*): he should identify himself (*attatāya*) with all (*sabbesu*), be they inferior, middling, or superior, be they friends, foes, or indifferent, etc. It means that he should regard them as the same as himself, without making the distinction that they are 'other beings.' Or, the term may mean (simply), 'with all one's heart,' without leaving out even the least bit of it. *Far-reaching* refers to the width of suffusion. It is *gone great* on account of its (high jhanic) level. It is *unlimited* on account of the dexterity involved (in including every living being), and because it has an unlimited number of beings for its object.

(*3e. Variations*): Only those who have achieved full concentration can practise the following three methods given in the Patisambhidā:

I. In these *five ways* there is an *undifferentiated* suffusion of the friendliness which sets the heart free, *i.e.*, 'May 1. all beings be free from enmity, injury, and disturbance, and may they preserve themselves at ease! May 2. all that breathes, 3. all creatures, 4. all persons, 5. all those counted as individuals, be free from enmity, etc.!

II. In these *seven ways* there is a *specified* suffusion of the friendliness which sets the heart free, *i.e.*, 'May 1. all women be free from enmity, etc.! May 2. all men, 3. all the saints, 4. all the common people, 5. all the gods, 6. all human beings, 7. all those in the states of woe, be free from enmity, etc.!'

III. There is thirdly the friendliness, which sets the heart free, and which carries out a suffusion *in the ten directions in ten ways, i.e.*, '(A) May all beings 1. in the East be free from enmity, etc.! May all beings in 2. the West, 3. the North, 4. the South, 5. the North-East, 6. the North-West, 7. the South-West, 8. the South-East, 9. above, and 10. below, be free from enmity, etc.! May all that breathes, all creatures, all persons, all those included within the realm of individual existence 1. in the East, . . . 10. below, be free from enmity, etc.! (B) May all women 1. in the East . . . 10. below be free from enmity, etc.! May all men, saints, common people, gods, humans, and damned 1. in the East . . . 2. below be free from enmity, etc.!'

### c. Unlimited Compassion

First of all he should direct his compassion on a man whom he sees to be pitiable, deformed, in extreme distress, ill-fated, ill-favoured, and wretched, with mutilated hands and feet, with a begging bowl in front of him, sitting in a rest-house for the poor, with plenty of vermin oozing from his limbs, and uttering moans of distress. And the disciple should think, 'Alas, this man has fallen on evil days! Good were it if he were freed from this suffering!'

If no one like that is met with, compassion should be aroused for an evil-doer. Even though he may seem at ease, actually he is like a condemned criminal. And how? There the king's men lead a robber caught in the act, on the orders of the king that he should be executed, in bonds to the place of execution, and deal out to him a hundred lashes at each cross road. Humane bystanders give him something to eat and to chew, as well as flowers, perfumes, ointments and betel leaves. Although eating and enjoying these things, he walks along as if he were happy and a man of great wealth, nevertheless nobody would actually imagine him to be happy and rich; on the contrary people pity him, and say, 'this poor fellow is sure to die soon; each step brings him nearer to his death.' Just so the monk, who practises the meditation on compassion, may feel compassion even for a happy person, and think: 'Although this poor fellow at present is happy and well-provided, and enjoys his possessions, he will nevertheless, in the absence of any wholesome deeds done through even one of the three doors of action (*i.e.*, by body, speech or mind), soon experience not a little pain and sadness in the states of woe.'

When he has learned to feel compassion for that person, he should in the same way direct his compassion first on 2. a dear person, then 3. an indifferent person, and then 4. an enemy.

### *d. Unlimited sympathetic joy*

A very dear friend is here a suitable basis, one who in the Commentary is called a friend intoxicated with joy. He is one who is exceedingly joyful, alternatively laughs and talks away. Therefore he should first of all be suffused with sympathetic joy. Or, when the disciple sees or hears that a person dear to him is happy, well-off, and joyful, he should produce sympathetic joy, and think: 'How joyous that being is! How good! How splendid!' But if that friend who is intoxicated with joy, or if the dear person, have been happy in the past, but just now are ill-fated and ill-favoured, one should recall only their happy condition in the past, and produce sympathetic joy, by taking account only of their joyous state in the past, and think: 'Once in the past he had such great wealth, so great retinue, and he was always joyful.' And one should also produce sympathetic joy by taking account of his joyous state in the future, and think: 'In the future he will again regain his prosperity, and he will move along on the backs of elephants, on horseback, in golden palanquins, and so on.' When one has in this way produced sympathetic joy for the dear person, one must then direct one's sympathetic joy successively on an indifferent person, and then on an enemy.

### *e. Unlimited Evenmindedness*

But if the disciple wants to develop the meditation on evenmindedness, he must first acquire the third or fourth trance with friendliness. When he has emerged from the third Jhāna, after becoming quite familiar with it, he should see the dangers of the first three states,—*i.e.*, that the wish 'may they be happy, etc.' may be connected with an attention involving fondness for beings, that (with compassion) he moves very near to repugnance and affection, and that (with sympathetic joy) devotion to gladness may lead to coarseness. In addition he should see the advantages of the evenmindedness, which consists in quiet calm. He then should produce evenmindedness, first of all towards a person who is naturally indifferent to him, and upon him he should look impartially. After he has, in the manner just described, produced evenmindedness for an indifferent person, then for a dear person, then for a friend intoxicated with joy, and then for an enemy, he should break down the barriers by being equally indifferent towards all these and himself, and he should cultivate that mental image, develop it, and frequently repeat it. When he acts like that, the fourth stage of Jhāna will arise.

## 3. THE EVOCATION OF DEITIES

### *The Evocation of Tārā*

(*Preliminaries*): The officiant should first of all wash his face, feet, etc. When thus purified he should be seated at his ease in a solitary place, which is strewn with fragrant flowers and pervaded by pleasant scents, and which is agreeable to him.

In his own heart he should conceive the moon's orb as evolved from the primal sound A. In the centre of it he should visualize a beautiful blue lotus, then the moon's unspotted orb within its filaments, and further thereon the yellow germ-syllable TĀṂ. Sheafs of lustrous rays issue from that yellow germ syllable TĀṂ and they dispel the darkness of the world's delusions and illuminate the boundless world systems in all the ten directions. All these he makes shine downwards, and he educes from them the countless Buddhas and Bodhisattvas whose abode is there. These Buddhas and Bodhisattvas are then established on the background of the firmament.

1. He then first performs the great *worship* of these greatly compassionate Buddhas and Bodhisattvas who are established on the background of the firmament, with celestial flowers, incense, perfumes, garlands, unguents, aromatic powders, garments, umbrellas, flags, bells, banners, and the like.

2. After that he should make a *confession of his sins*, as follows: 'Whatever evil acts I may have done, caused to be done, or consented to be done, in the course of my wanderings through this beginningless samsaric world, whether with my body, or my mind, all these I confess and I will abstain from them in the future. And he should also include a promise of greater zeal with regard to the virtuous deeds which he has been wont to leave undone.

3. After that he should perform the *Rejoicing at Merit,* as follows: 'I rejoice at the entire mass of meritorious deeds of the Sugatas, of the Pratyekabuddhas, of the Disciples, of the Bodhisattvas who are the Jina's sons, and of all the world with its Gods and with its Brahmas.'

4. Then comes the *Taking of Refuge in the Three Treasures:* 'I take refuge in the Buddha, in the Dharma, in the Samgha,—until the time that I myself will have reached the terrace of enlightenment.'

5. Then comes the act of *Adhesion to the Path:* 'It is for me to adhere to the Path indicated by the Tathagatas, and to none other.'

6. Then the *Entreaty:* 'May the Blessed Tathagatas and their sons (the Bodhisattvas), who have worked for

the world's weal since its first beginning, stand by and effect my final Nirvana.'

7. Then the *Petition:* 'May the Blessed Tathagatas indoctrinate me with incomparable expositions of the Dharma, of such a kind that beings in the samsaric world may quite soon be set free from the bondage of becoming.'

8. Then he should make a *Dedication of Merit:* 'Whatever meritoriousness may have arisen by the performance of the sevenfold extraordinary office and by the confession of sins, all that I dedicate to the attainment of full enlightenment (by all beings).' Or he recites the verses which describe the sevenfold extraordinary office:

'All sins I confess, and I gladly rejoice in the merits of others.
So that I may not linger in the state of birth, I take refuge in the Blessed One,
In the Dharma, in all the Three Treasures. To enlightenment I give over my thoughts.
I adhere to His Path, and I dedicate my merits to the attainment of full enlightenment.'

As soon as he has celebrated the sevenfold extraordinary office, he should pronounce the formula of dismissal: OṂ ĀḤ MŪḤ. Or, alternatively he should recite:

'Our limbs anointed with the Santal ointment of morality,
Covered with the garments of the trances,
Strewn with the lotus flowers of the limbs of enlightenment,
We have dwelt at ease and in happiness.'

9. Thereupon he should develop in due order the four *Stations of Brahma, i.e.*, friendliness, compassion, sympathetic joy and evenmindedness.

10. After he has realized the four Stations of Brahmā, he should develop (the insight into) the *perfect purity of the original nature of all dharmas.* For 'all dharmas by their nature and own-being are perfectly pure, and also I have a nature which is perfectly pure,'—this insight he should realize directly and face to face. And this fact that all dharmas are by their nature perfectly pure should be established by the following mantra: 'Oṃ, pure in their own-being are all the dharmas, pure in my own-being am I.' But if all dharmas are perfectly pure in their original nature, what is it then that brings to pass this samsaric world? The reason is that it has been covered up with the impurities of the notions of subject and object, and so forth. The expedient that leads to their removal is the development of the true Path. For through that may it be stopped. It is thus that one achieves insight into the perfect natural purity of all dharmas.

11. After he has meditated on the perfect natural purity of all dharmas, the officiant should meditate on the *emptiness of all dharmas.* And this here is meant by emptiness: The universe, whether in motion or at rest, is in itself nothing but a clear non-dual Shine, which has become obscured by all these deceptive imaginings, such as subject and object, and so on. On that he should reflect. And this emptiness he should establish by the following mantra: 'Oṃ, Through my cognition of emptiness I myself am essentially of adamantine own-being.'

12. Then he should meditate on the *Blessed Lady, the Holy Tārā,* as proceeding from the yellow germ-syllable TĀṂ, which stands on the spotless orb of the moon, which again is inside the filaments of the full blown lotus, which is within the lunar orb originally established on the heart. He should conceive her to be of deep green colour, two-armed, with a smiling face, proficient in every virtue, without defect of any kind, adorned with orna-

ments of heavenly gold, rubies, pearls and jewels; her twin breasts decorated with lovely garlands, her two arms decked with heavenly bracelets and bangles, her loins beautified with glittering rows of girdles of flawless gems, her two ankles beautified by golden anklets set with divers gems, her hair entwined with fragrant wreaths made of the flowers of the paradise tree and others of that kind, with the figure of the Lord Amoghasiddhi, the Tathagata, in her resplendent jewelled headdress,—a radiant and most seductive similitude, in the prime of her youth, with eyes of the blue of the autumn lotus, her body robed in heavenly garments, in the Arddhaparyanka posture, within a circle of white rays on a white lotus as large as a cart-wheel, her right hand in the sign of generosity (*varadā*), and holding in her left a full blown blue lotus. Let him develop this likeness of our Blessed Lady as long as he wishes.

Thereupon our eternally perfect Blessed Lady is led forth out of space, in her intelligible aspect, by means of the numerous sheafs of rays which illumine the triple world, and which issue from the yellow germ-syllable TĀṂ, which is in the filaments of the lotus in the moon of which the orb was established on the heart, and from that Blessed Lady (herself). When he has led her forth and established her on the background of the firmament, he should offer an oblation at the feet of that Blessed Lady, with scented water and fragrant flowers in a jewelled vessel, and should then offer a respectful welcome (lit. worship) to her in many ways, with heavenly flowers, incense, scents, garlands, unguents, aromatic powders, garments, umbrellas, flags, bells, banners, and so forth. After he has thus again and again worshipped, and lauded her, he should exhibit the appropriate finger-sign called 'the open lotus flower' (which is then described). After he has, with this finger-sign, gratified our

Blessed Lady's intelligible aspect, he should develop the incantation (mantra) in relation to her contingent aspect. And he should resolutely believe in the non-duality of those two aspects.

Thereupon the rays which issue from the germ-syllable TĀṂ that is upon the spotless orb of the moon within the filaments of the blue lotus in the lunar orb,—rays that are of unlimited range, proper to the divine Tārā, and that illuminate the ten quarters of the triple world, —now take away the poverty and other ills of beings who live in this triple world, by means of showers of manifold jewels which rain down from above, and they refresh them with the nectar of the teachings of the Dharma, which reveals all things as impermanent, without self, and so forth. After he has thus concerned himself with the divers needs of the world, he should evolve in his meditation also the cosmic aspect of Tārā. Again he should meditate, until tired, on whatever has come to be in the yellow germ-syllable TĀṂ, in the stages of expansion and contraction. If he gets exhausted from his meditation, he should murmur the mantra, which is here OṂ TĀRE TUTTĀRE TURE SVĀHĀ. This truly royal mantra is of great power. All Tathagatas have honoured, worshipped and revered it.

When he has emerged from the trance, the Yogin, who has seen the whole universe in the form of Tārā, should dwell at will conscious of his own identity with the Blessed Lady.

(*Benefits*): When someone meditates on the Blessed Lady in this manner, the eight great magical proficiencies fall at his feet. What need is there to speak of the other, lesser, proficiencies, which come to him as a matter of course. Whoever meditates on our Blessed Lady in a lonely mountain cave, he will behold her face to face with his own eyes. And the Blessed Lady herself bestows upon him his very respiration, and all else. Not to say any more, she puts the very Buddhahood, so hard to win, into the very palm of his hand.

# IV

# WISDOM

## I. THE FOUR HOLY TRUTHS

### *a. The truth of ill*

*'Birth is ill.'* Why then is birth regarded as ill? Because it is the basis of a great variety of ills. Seven varieties of ill can, indeed, be distinguished, *i.e.:*

1. 'The ill which consists in pain,'—these are the mental and physical painful feelings, which are ill both by nature and in name.

2. 'The ill from reversal,'—when a pleasant feeling is reversed, it becomes the cause of the arising of ill.

3. 'The ill of conditioned things,'—in so far as indifferent feelings, as well as all the other conditioned things on the three planes of existence, are oppressed by rise and fall.

4. 'Hidden ill,' refers to physical afflictions such as sharp pains in the ears or teeth, or mental afflictions such as the feverish pain born of passion or hate, in those cases when one can recognize (the reason why someone seems to suffer) only by making enquiries, and when (the occasion which causes) the attack is not apparent. It is also called 'non-apparent ill.'

5. 'Unconcealed ill,'—these are the afflictions brought about by the 32 kinds of torture, since they are recognizable even without making enquiries, and (the occasion which causes) the attack is apparent. It is also called 'apparent ill.'

6. 'Indirect ill,'—this refers to all the kinds of ill, with the exception of the ill which consists in pain; *i.e.*, to birth, etc., which are the basis of this or that ill. But the ill which consists in pain is called 'direct ill.'

And here birth is ill because it is the basis of (a) the sufferings of the states of woe which the Lord has revealed by way of simile in the Sutra about the Wise and the Fool (M 129; iii 165 *sq.*), and others; and (b) of the ill which arises even to one who has a happy destiny in the world of men, and which is rooted in the descent into the womb, the experiences during one's stay in the womb, in miscarriages, the act of birth, and the shocks one has to undergo immediately after birth. (All these are described in detail in nos. 37–41.) (c) In addition there is the ill rooted in attacks on oneself. In the course of their life those suffer this kind of ill who kill themselves, or, in the manner of the Naked Ascetics, and others, give themselves up to self-torture and self-castigation, or in their anger refuse to eat, or hang themselves up. (d) By contrast, ill rooted in the attacks of others is that which arises in someone who experiences the pains of being killed, beaten or fettered by others. And thus birth is the basis for all these ills.

*'Sickness is ill. Old age is ill.'* And old age is ill (a) in that it is one of the ills (characteristic) of conditioned things (see 3 above), and (b) because it is the basis of ills. It is the basis of the physical and mental sufferings which arise as a result of many and various things such as the loosening of all the limbs, the disturbance of the sense-faculties, unsightliness, loss of youth, debility, impairment of memory and judgment, and the contempt of others.

*'Death is ill.'* 'The evil man discerns (at the hour of

death) the evil deeds (he has committed during his life), or an indication of his evil destiny (in his next life); the good man who cannot bear to be separated from the things dear to him: whatever mental ill there is in one who is dying, and whatever, in addition, there is by way of physical suffering, unendurable and irreparable, such as the tearing apart of the joints and sinews, and the pressure on the soft and vital spots of the body,—for all these ills it is this death which constitutes the basis. It is therefore that death has been called an ill.'

*'To be conjoined with what one dislikes means suffering. To be disjoined from what one likes means suffering. Not to get what one wants, also that means suffering.'*

*'In short, all grasping at (any of) the five skandhas (involves) suffering.'* Birth, and so on, oppress the five grasping skandhas in many ways, just as in the case of the fire and the fuel, the weapons and the target, gadflies, mosquitoes, etc., and a cow's body, the reapers and the field, robbers and a village. And they are brought forth in the grasping skandhas just as grass, creepers, etc., grow on the ground, or flowers, fruits and sprouts on trees.

But even in the course of many aeons it would not be possible to enumerate all this suffering in detail or to do justice to it. In order therefore to demonstrate all this ill, the Lord has summed it up in these five grasping skandhas, just as the taste of all the water in the whole ocean can be found in a single drop of seawater, and He has said: 'in short, the five grasping skandhas are ill.'

### *b. The sixteen aspects*

There are sixteen aspects of the four holy truths, and it is by wisdom that they are understood. They are:

*I. For the fact of Ill*

1. *Impermanent,* because things rise up in dependence on causes.

2. *Ill,* because by their very nature they are oppressive.

3. *Empty,* because they do not bear out the view that anything belongs to a self.

4. *Impersonal,* because they do not bear out the view that there is a self.

*II. For the fact of Origination*

5. *Cause,* in so far as things are due to a number of remote causes.

6. *Origination,* in so far as they become manifest as a result of their proximate causes.

7. *Product,* because they are, as a series of momentary dharmas, subject to successive acts of causation.

8. *Condition,* in so far as they are achieved by the concord of many conditions.

*III. For the fact of Stopping*

9. *Stopping,* because (in Nirvana) the skandhas have become extinct.

10. *Calm quietude,* because the three fires,—of greed, hate and delusion,—have become extinct.

11. *Sublime,* because there are here no misfortunes.

12. *Definite Escape,* because it is free from everything that may cause ill.

*IV. For the fact of the Path*

13. *The path,* in the sense that one walks along it towards Nirvana.

14. *Correct Method,* because it is both effective and expedient.

15. *Progress,* because it imparts Nirvana.

16. *Factor of Release,* because it can produce a definite going-forth (from this world).

There is, however, a second explanation:

1. *Impermanent,* because not perpetual.
2. *Ill,* because like a burden.
3. *Empty,* because void of such attributes of personality as being an agent, etc.
4. *Impersonal,* because uncontrollable.
5. *Cause,* in so far as things arise from it.
6. *Origination,* in so far as they emerge, as it were, from the future.
7. *Product,* in so far as they consist of interconnected processes.
8. *Condition,* when the chief factor in any given act of production is considered.
9. *Stopping,* because all past ill has been stilled, and future ill cannot take place.
10. *Calm Quietude,* because freed from rise, persistance and fall (the three marks of all conditioned things).
11. *Sublime,* because good in the ultimate sense.
12. *Definite Escape,* because it brings complete security and the highest possible consolation.
13. *Path,* because opposed to the wrong paths.
14. *Correct Method,* because opposed to wrong methods.
15. *Progress,* because it does not disappoint those who are on their way to the city of Nirvana.
16. *Factor of Release,* because it abandons the triple becoming.

Since the traditional explanations do not agree, we will offer a third one:

1. *Impermanent,* because it is born and perishes.

2. *Ill,* because it is repugnant to the thought of holy men.

3. *Empty,* because no self can be found in it.

4. *Impersonal,* because it is not a self.

5. *Cause,*—craving, in the sense of self-love, is the initial cause of all suffering, as the seed is the initial cause of the fruit.

6. *Origination,*—craving, in the sense of desire for re-birth, is the intermediate cause of suffering, as the production of shoot, stem, etc., is a causal process leading to the fruit.

7. *Product,*—craving, as the definite decision to win a definite rebirth, is the proximate cause of suffering, as the flower is the proximate cause of the fruit.

8. *Condition,*—craving, as the desire for a definite re-birth, is the subsidiary cause of suffering, as the soil, water, manure, etc., are the subsidiary causes of the fruit.

9. *Stopping,* because it cuts off the round of births.

10. *Calm Quietude,* as the termination of all ill.

11. *Sublime,* because nothing can be superior to it.

12. *Definite Escape,* because it is irreversible.

13. *Path,* because like a straight and direct road.

14. *Correct Method,* because in accordance with true reality.

15. *Progress,* because purity can be obtained by this path only, and by no other.

16. *Factor of Release,* because it separates definitely from the triple becoming.

There is still a fourth explanation. The aspects are then considered as antidotes to the following false views:

1. *Impermanent,* the view that there are things which are permanent.

2. *Ill,* the view that happiness can be found in conditioned things.

3. *Empty,* the view that anything belongs to a self.

4. *Impersonal,* the view that there is a self.

5. *Cause,* the view that there is no cause.

6. *Origination,* the view that there is only one single cause, such as God (Ishvara).

7. *Product,* the view that entities evolve or can undergo transformation.

8. *Condition,* the view that the world is created by an intelligent being.

9. *Stopping,* the view that no deliverance is possible.

10. *Calm Quietude,* the view that deliverance consists in pain and suffering.

11. *Sublime,* the view that the happiness of the trances is the sublimest thing of all.

12. *Definite Escape,* the view that deliverance is not definite, that one can fall away from it.

13. *Path,* the view that there is no Path.

14. *Correct Method,* the view that a wrong path is the right one.

15. *Progress,* the view that there is another path.

16. *Factor of Release,* the view that the path may fail us.

## 2. THE THREE MARKS OF CONDITIONED THINGS

### *a. The 165 Considerations*

This is the arrangement with regard to the skandhas: 'Whatever form there is, all that he determines as impermanent. This is one separate consideration. He determines it as ill, as not self. These are two more separate considerations.'

This monk then classifies all form, indicated indefinitely as 'whatever form,' from 11 points of view,—the triplet of past, present and future, and the four pairs of inward-outward, gross-refined, low-exalted, distant-near. 'He determines all form as impermanent,' considers it as impermanent. In the following manner, as it has been stated : ' Form, whether, past, present, or future, is impermanent in the sense of becoming extinct.'

He considers impermanence in the sense of extinction as follows : Past form is impermanent in the sense of becoming extinct because it got extinct already in the past, and has not gone on to this (present) becoming. Future form is impermanent in the sense of becoming extinct because it will come into being in the immediately following becoming, and just there it will become extinct, and not go to a further becoming after that. Present form is impermanent in the sense of becoming extinct because it becomes extinct even now and does not go hence. Inward form is impermanent in the sense of becoming extinct because it gets extinct (even) as just inward, and does not go on to a state where it is outward. And so for the four pairs, until we come to : Near form is impermanent in the sense of becoming extinct because it gets extinct just there, and does not go on to a state where it is far. That all this is impermanent in the sense of extinction, is, in this way, one single consideration, but broken up it is elevenfold.

And all this is *ill* in the sense of being fearful, because it is dangerous. For what is impermanent, that brings fear. The gods (trembled when the Tathagata reminded them of their impermanence in the Sīhopama-sutra.) That this is ill in the sense of being fearful is one single consideration, but broken up it is elevenfold.

And as all this is ill, so it is *not-self* in the sense of being without substance, because there is no self-substance which is imagined as a self, an indweller, a doer, a feeler, one having power over his own. For what is impermanent that is ill, and unable to hold back its own impermanence, or its molestation by rise and fall. Whence therefore its position as a doer, etc.? Hence it is said: 'If, oh monks, this form were the self, this form would not be liable to oppression' (S iii 66), and so on. That this is not-self in the sense of being without substance is one single consideration, but broken up it is again elevenfold.

The same method should be applied to feelings, perceptions, impulses, and consciousness.

But because what is impermanent is assuredly 'Compounded,' etc., therefore, in order to show its implications, or to direct the attention in various ways, the text states again: 'Form, past, future and present, is impermanent, compounded, produced in dependance on conditioned co-production, doomed to extinction, doomed to fall, fit for dispassion, fit for cessation' (S iii 24).

The same method should be applied to feelings, etc.

### *b. The three marks defined*

All the conditioned processes which take place in the interval between birth and death are *impermanent*. How? Because rise and fall take place, because of their reversal, because they last out no more than their time, and because they are opposite to permanence. But since the conditioned processes which have arisen reach stability, are during their stability worn out by decay, and, on reaching decay, inevitably break up, therefore they are also *ill*, owing to the fact that they are constantly molested (by rise and fall), that they are hard to bear, that they are the basis of suffering, and that they are opposite to Ease. And they are also *not-self*, in so far as they are empty, under no master, powerless, and as opposite to the self; for they are empty of the ability to wield power in the sense that there is no one who has power over these three positions, and can say: 'Let those conditioned processes which have arisen not reach stability! Let those which have reached stability not decay! Let those which have reached decay not break up!'

### 3. SURVEY OF CONDITIONS

#### *a. The range of conditioning*

(*Two conditions of the fivefold sense-consciousness.*) What is that form which is the sense-field of vision? (a) the eye, the sentient organ, derived from the four great primaries, included in the personality, invisible and reacting,—the eye, invisible and reacting, by which one has seen, sees, will, or may see form that is visible and reacting (impingeing); . . .

(b) (In the case of involuntary vision): The eye . . . reacting,—the eye, invisible and reacting, against which form that is visible and reacting, has impinged, impinges, will, or may impinge;

(c) (In the case of voluntary looking): The eye . . . reacting,—the eye, invisible and reacting, which has impinged, impinges, will, or may impinge, on from that is visible and reacting.

(d) The eye . . . reacting,—dependent on that eye, with reference to a sight-stimulus, 1. a visual contact has arisen, arises, will, or may arise; 2. a feeling, 3. a perception, 4. a volition, 5. (an act of) visual consciousness; (and further), dependent on that eye, with a (visible) form for object, there has arisen, arises, will, or may arise, 6. a visual contact, 7. a feeling, 8. a perception, 9. a volition, 10. (an act of) visual consciousness.

And so for the other four kinds of sensory consciousness, with the following alterations:

II. The ear . . . sounds that are invisible and reacting

(and so for the others) . . . auditory contact . . . auditory consciousness.

III. The nose . . . smells . . . olfactory contact . . . olfactory consciousness.

IV. The tongue . . . tastes . . . gustatory contact . . . gustatory consciousness.

V. The body . . . touchables . . . body-contact . . . body-consciousness.

(*Four conditions for an act of the sixfold sensory consciousness*) : For the elements of visual consciousness, etc., not only the eye and form, etc., are the conditions, but also light, etc. Hence the ancient masters have said : 'An act of visual consciousness arises conditioned by eye, (visible) form, light and attention. An act of auditory consciousness arises conditioned by ear, sound, a free access of sound (waves) to the inner ear, and attention. An act of olfactory consciousness arises conditioned by nose, smell, the air (which carries the stimulus along), and attention. An act of gustatory consciousness arises conditioned by tongue, taste, the water (moisture, in which the stimulus is carried), and attention. An act of body-consciousness arises conditioned by body, touchables, the solidity (which must characterize the stimulus), and attention. An act of mind-consciousness arises conditioned by subconsciousness (*bhavanga*), mind, a mind-object and attention. (The Vimuttimagga here gives, better : mind, mind-object, intentness (*adhimokkha*), and attention.)

(*Five conditions for an act of visual consciousness*) : 'Dependent on (at least) five factors does eye-consciousness come into being : there must be the eye as the subjective (inner) support ; form as the objective (outer) support ; light to illuminate the form, or to make it visible ; an unobstructed field of vision, between eye and form ; appropriate attention to direct the mental processes to the situation. When any of these factors is absent, or rendered ineffective by other conditions, eye-consciousness is not produced. From the combination of these five factors does the production of eye-consciousness result. (*And so for the other senses.*)

(*Four conditions for an act of visual consciousness*): Visual consciousness takes place for four reasons, *i.e.*, 1. One seizes on external objects, and does not understand that they are nothing but his own Mind. 2. One settles down in forms and habit energy accumulated since beginningless time by false reasoning and depravity. 3. The own-being inherent in the nature of consciousness. 4. The eagerness for multiple forms and their characteristics. (*And so for the other senses.*)

### *b. The automatic nature of conditioning*

(*With regard to the sense-fields*): They should be seen correctly, and regarded as inactive (without inward striving) and as unpreoccupied. For eye-and-form, etc., do not think thus: 'May consciousness arise out of our concord!' Nor do they, by their existence as doors (of the senses=sense-organs), bases and objects, strain themselves so that consciousness should be produced, nor do they occupy themselves (with that task). But it is in the course of events that out of the concord between eye and form, etc., visual consciousness, etc., should come about.

There it does not occur to the eye: 'I do for visual consciousness the work of being its subjective support'; to form it does not occur, 'I do for visual consciousness the work of being its objective support'; to light it does not occur: 'I do for visual consciousness the work of illumination'; to space it does not occur, 'I do for visual consciousness the work of providing an unobstructed field of vision'; to the appropriate attention it does not occur, 'I do for visual consciousness the work of directing the mind to the situation'; and to visual consciousness it does not occur, 'I have been generated by those conditions.' But when these conditions are there, the genesis and manifestation of visual consciousness takes place. And so one should work it out for the other senses.

(*With regard to mind and body*): This should be regarded as follows: Just as a wooden doll is empty, lifeless and without inner striving, and yet it walks and stands up when the strings are pulled which are fastened on to it, and it appears to be full of activity and occupied with doing things; just so this psycho-physical organism is empty, lifeless and without inner striving, and yet it walks and stands up because the one (the body) is conjoined with the other (the mind), and it appears to be full of activity and occupied with doing things. As the Ancients have said:

'In truth there is here only name and form,
And there exists here neither living being nor man.
Void is it, and constructed like a puppet,
A mass of misery, and like wood or straw.'

### *c. Conditioned co-production*

The classical formulation of this doctrine states that 12 factors condition each other, in the sense that both their origination and their cessation is linked together. The formula is common to all Buddhists, but the explanations differ in the various schools. Here, following Buddhaghosa, I give a summary of the Theravadin interpretation. A diagram shows the subdivisions of each link, and their representations in art.

The word 'conditioned' is here said to mean 'where this is that becomes.' This rule applies to all conditioned events, but in the formula of conditioned co-production interest is concentrated on the chain of rebirths. It explains not so much the world, as the possibilities of salvation from it. The formula aims at tracing the most essential conditions which govern our lives as individuals in this samsaric world, and prevent us from gaining the freedom of Nirvana.

Now to the twelve links themselves. First of all, what is 1. *ignorance?* It is of two kinds, (a) non-attainment of knowledge, or blindness, and (b) the production of false knowledge, *i.e.*, deception or self-deception. (a) We are blind in so far as we have no knowledge of what exists in the ultimate sense, and ignorant of the dharmas, of their general marks (impermanence, ill, not-self), of Nirvana, and of the facts taught in the four holy truths. (b) We are self-deceived in so far as we turn to a manufactured world of our own making, which covers up and conceals the true world, to which wisdom alone can penetrate. Blind to the skandhas, etc., we react to fictitious units, such as 'men,' 'women,' 'things,' etc., which ultimately do not exist. It is amongst them that we seek for the permanence, happiness and full control which are found only in Nirvana. But this Nirvana is hidden from our sight by the multiplicity of persons and things. This is the definition of ignorance.

2. The *karma-formations* are that which 'puts together the compounded.' They are classified as meritorious, demeritorious, and imperturbable (found in the formless trances), and they consist of deeds of body, speech or mind. In this context only those volitions are considered which produce rebirth. Those which are karmically neutral, or peculiar to the Arhat, are left out of account. How then does ignorance condition the karma-forma-

tions? A consideration of the difference between the actions of an Arhat and those of an ordinary person makes the connection quite clear: The Arhat acts without a belief in self, free from greed, hate and delusion, and with an insight into the four holy truths. An ordinary person, on the contrary, acts from a wrong belief in self, and ignores the four holy truths. His actions are therefore obviously linked to ignorance, and that is the reason why he is reborn again and again. The Arhat, on the other hand, has escaped the necessity for rebirth.

Factors 1 and 2 are held to refer to the past life. Now we advance to a new existence, the present life. 3. *Consciousness* here means 'rebirth-consciousness,' *i.e.,* the consciousness which arises at the very moment of conception. The last mental act of the previous life, the 'decease consciousness,' is followed by a mental act which initiates a new existence in a new body. Non-Buddhists are inclined to believe that conception is an involuntary act, imposed upon us by what our parents did. Here it is assumed that it is essentially a voluntary act, the result of what we ourselves have been doing in the past. The deeds of our past life are held to determine the nature of the act of consciousness which exists at conception. This act of consciousness is further regarded as the nucleus round which a new personality is organized, as a kind of 'psychic embryo.' Of the five skandhas, consciousness is likely to be the one which forms the centre of a new being, because it is the central act of awareness by which an individual is set up as a conscious subject against the rest of the world.

4. *Name-and-form* is another word for the five skandhas,—'form' being the first, and 'name' the four others. 'Name-and-form' is a somewhat archaic term for the psycho-physical organism, which is now settling down and coagulating round the nucleus of consciousness. Con-

sciousness and name-and-form are said to depend on each other like two bundles of reed, leaning one against the other.

The psycho-physical organism obviously is a necessary condition for the arising of 5. the *six sense-fields*. This term comprises (a) the six sense-organs, with mind as the sixth; (b) the six fields, or objects, of the senses; and (c) the six consciousnesses attached to the sense-organs.

These three obviously make 6. *contact* possible, which is defined as the collocation, or meeting, or coinciding, of organ, object and consciousness. 'Dependent on eye and forms arises eye-consciousness; the concourse of the three is contact.'

Contact again is a necessary condition of 7. *feeling*, which is of three kinds,—pleasant, unpleasant, and neutral.

Feeling in its turn leads to 8. *craving:* A pleasant feeling makes us wish to have more of this experience; unpleasant feeling leads to a desire for release from it, or makes us crave for sense-enjoyment which would counteract it; neutral feeling, a kind of peaceful calm, again makes us desire more of it.

9. *Grasping* is just a hardened form of craving, hardened either by greater intensity, and a firmer seizure of sense-objects, or by an acceptance of, or infusion with, perverted views. 'Craving is desire for an object not yet attained, like the hand of a thief stretched out in the dark. Grasping is the seizing of an object that is attained, like the seizing of treasure by the thief.' Four kinds of grasping are distinguished: (a) We may grasp at sense-objects, hoping to derive delight or security from them. Or we may grasp at false opinions, of which again three kinds are distinguished: (b) First there are the views which preclude any hope of salvation,—materialistic views, nihilistic views, and so on. (c) Secondly there are

the views which expect salvation to result from practices which cannot produce it. And thirdly there is (d) the gasping at the word 'self,' covering all the thinking and speaking in which we use the word 'I' or its derivatives. These three kinds of views are here mentioned because they so greatly contribute to our enslavement by sense-objects. Without such perverted views we would be more inclined to give them up.

It is at this stage that something practical can be done to break the chain. Faced with craving we can transmute it into serene faith, and thus secure a better rebirth. And grasping can be impeded when we see that we always grasp at something which is not suitable to providing a lasting or full satisfaction.

The last three links are held to refer to a new, *i.e.*, the next or future, existence. 10. *Becoming* is of two kinds. There is (a) 'karma-becoming,'—either wholesome or unwholesome. This is just another term for the deeds which condition rebirth, and identical with no. 2 (karma-formations). (b) 'Rebirth-becoming' is the reactive side of the process, the effect. That is considered here, and in particular the plane within the triple world into which his past karma propels the individual, who may be reborn in the formless world, the world of form, or the world of sense-desire. In the latter he has a choice between Gods, Asuras, men, ghosts, animals and infernal beings.

11. *Birth* here covers the growth of the skandhas during the pre-natal period, in the interval between conception and the ejection of the foetus. For beings who are not born from a womb, the concept must be modified accordingly.

12. *Decay and Death* is the necessary outcome of birth. Birth is the cause of death. All the circumstances, or efficient causes, which may bring about the actual

event of death are but its occasions. The act of birth is the decisive cause which makes death inevitable, before a bus or a bullet give us the final push. Birth implies death, as its necessary consequence. Conversely, no birth, no death. That is what we hope to attain when striving for immortality, the goal of all Buddhist meditation.

## CONDITIONED CO-PRODUCTION

| | | | |
|---|---|---|---|
| PAST LIFE<br>Karma-process:<br>Past Causes | 1. Ignorance | (a) Blindness<br>(b) Self-deception | Blind man feeling his way with a stick |
| | 2. Karmic Activities | (a) meritorious<br>(b) demeritorious<br>(c) imperturbable | Potter with wheel and pots |
| | (decease-consciousness) | | |
| PRESENT LIFE<br>Rebirth-process:<br>Present Effects | 3. (Rebirth-)Consciousness | | Monkey climbing a tree with flowers |
| | 4. Name-and-form (psycho-physical organism) | (a) form<br>(b) feelings<br>(c) perceptions<br>(d) impulses<br>(e) consciousness | A ship with four passengers, consciousness steering |
| | 5. Six sense-fields | (a) 6 sense-organs<br>(b) 6 sense-objects<br>(c) 6 kinds of sense-consciousness | Empty house with six windows |
| | 6. Contact | (a) eye-contact, etc. to<br>(e) mind-contact | Man with arrow in his eye |
| | 7. Feeling | (a) pleasant<br>(b) unpleasant<br>(c) neutral | Man and woman embracing |
| Karma-process:<br>Present Causes | 8. Craving | (a) for sense pleasures<br>(b) for existence<br>(c) for non-existence | Woman offers drink to seated man |
| | 9. Grasping | (a) at sense-objects<br>(b) at wrong views<br>(c) at mere rule and ritual | Man picking fruit from tree |
| | (karma-becoming) | (d) at the word 'self' | |
| FUTURE LIFE<br>Rebirth-process:<br>Future Effects | 10. (Rebirth-) Becoming | (a) realm of sense-desire<br>(b) realm of form<br>(c) formless realm | Woman with child |
| | 11. (Conception and) Birth | | Woman in child birth |
| | 12. Decay and Death | | Man carrying corpse to cemetery |

## 4. WITHDRAWAL FROM THE WORLD
## THE EIGHT COGNITIONS

### *1. The reviewing of rise and fall*

'The cognition of the reviewing of rise and fall is the wise reviewing of the reversal of present dharmas' (Pts I\ 1).

*1.1.* The disciple begins by way of the *summary method.* As the canonical text has it (Pts i 54): 'By "present" is meant here form which has arisen, feeling which has arisen, and so for the other skandhas, for sense-organs and sense-objects. The fact of their genesis is the "rise," the fact of their reversal is the "fall." The reviewing is the "cognition." ' In accordance with this canonical method, he reviews, with regard to all material and mental phenomena which have arisen, the fact of their genesis as their birth, production, new formation, or rise, and the fact of their reversal as their extinction, breaking-up, or fall.

*1.2.* He wisely knows: Before the arising of this material or mental phenomenon, that is to say, before they had been produced, there was no heap or accumulation of them. When they are being produced, there is no coming from such a heap or accumulation. And when they are being stopped, there is no going to this or that direction. And for those that have stopped there is no position where they could be placed by way of a heap, accumulation, or hoard. For the sound which is produced when a lute is played there has been no accumulation of itself which would precede its production; when it is being produced it does not come from some accumulation; when it stops it does not go away in this or that direction; and when it has stopped it does not persist anywhere by way of accumulation: but, dependent on the lute and its neck and a man's suitable effort, the sound becomes without having been, and, having been, disappears again. In this way also all dharmas, material and immaterial, without having been become, and, having been, disappear again.

*1.3.* The disciple further considers *in greater detail,* with reference to condition and to moment, that 'this is the rise of form, this is the fall of form; thus form rises, thus form passes away.' He considers here 50 marks, 10 for each skandha (Pts I 55–7); as follows: He sees the rise of the skandha form by way of the origination of its conditions, i.e., that the origination of form is conditioned by the origination of 1. ignorance, 2. craving, 3. karma, 4. nutriment; and so for the other skandhas, except that for feeling, perception, and impulses the fourth condition is 'contact,' and for consciousness 'name-and-form.' He sees the rise of the skandha form (etc.) when he sees 5. the fact of its genesis. He sees the fall of the skandha form, etc., by way of the stopping of its conditions, i.e., that the stopping of form, etc., is conditioned by the stopping of 6. ignorance, 7. craving, 8. karma, 9. nutriment (or contact, or name-and-form, as the case may be). He sees the fall of the skandha form, etc., when he sees 10. the fact of its reversal. As he attends thus, the cognition becomes clearer and clearer that 'thus surely these dharmas become without having been before, and, having been, they disappear again.'

For this is his discernment of the rise and fall by way of *condition* that he sees that the origination of the skandhas is from the origination of ignorance, etc., and the stopping of the skandhas is from the stopping of ignorance, etc. And this is his discernment of the rise and fall by way of *moment* that he sees the rise and fall of the skandhas, when he sees the facts of their genesis and of their reversal; for the fact of genesis lies at the moment of their production, and the fact of reversal at the moment of their breaking-up.

As a result their actual own-being becomes obvious to him, for he looks through to the fact that it is circumscribed by their rise and fall. In this connection it also becomes obvious to him that what is conditioned can last only for a time, because he looks through to the fact that in the moment of rise the fall is absent, and the rise in the moment of fall. He understands: 'So, surely, these dharmas are produced, without having existed before, and, having been produced, they stop again.' The conditioned things which occur are always quite new (ones). And not only are they always quite new, they also have only a limited staying power, like a dewdrop at sunrise, like a water-bubble, like a line drawn with a stick in water, like a mustard seed resting on the point of an awl, or like a lightning flash. They also appear as unsubstantial, without substance, like a magical show, a mirage, a dream, a fire-wheel, a city of the Gandharvas, like foam, or a banana stem, etc.

*1.4.* Thus far he penetrates full fifty marks in this manner: 'It arises, but is doomed to fall; and when it has arisen it goes to its fall.'

*2. The reviewing of breaking-up*

As he persists in this practice, investigating and weighing up material and immaterial dharmas, the cognition works sharply in him, and their conditioned nature appears to him easily (and quickly). When his cognition works sharply in him, and their conditioned nature appears to him quickly, he does not attend to their production, or their persistence, or their proceeding, or their characteristics; his mindful attention is established only in their extinction, their fall, their breaking-up, their stopping. He sees that 'after these conditioned things have been produced they are stopped again.' . . . As it is said in the Patisambhidamagga (I 57): 'A thought with form for its object has arisen and is broken up again. Sizing up that object he reviews the breaking-up of that thought. And how then does he review it? He reviews it as impermanent, not permanent; as ill, not ease; as not the self, and not as the self; he turns away from it and does not delight in it; he loses his greed for it and does not long for it; he causes it (*i.e.*, greed) to stop, and not to arise; he casts it aside and does not cling to it. Reviewing it as impermanent, ill and not-self, he forsakes the notion of its permanence, happiness and selfhood. And so with feelings, and the other constituents of the personality.' As the Ancients have said:

> 'It is only skandhas which stop, and there is nothing else.
> The break-up of the skandhas is called death.
> The vigilant view their extinction,
> As when one cuts a jewel with a diamond.'

His attention further proceeds as follows: 'What had not yet stopped is stopping now, what had not yet broken up is breaking up.' He sees only just the breaking up, and with regard to all conditioned processes he pays no attention to their arising or their persistence, just as one does when one watches a fragile jar breaking, or fine dust being scattered, or sesamum seeds being fried. Just as a man who stands on the bank of a pond or a river sees, when big rain drops pour down, that on the surface of the water huge water-bubbles rise up, and as soon as they have arisen, rapidly break up again: even so he also sees that 'all conditioned processes break up, yes, they break up.' With regard to one who practises thus the Lord has said:

> 'Look on the world as if it were a bubble or a mirage.
> The King of Death cannot see him who views the world in such a way' (Dhp. 170).

*3. The cognition of the presence of danger*

As he thus tends, develops and increases the reviewing of the breaking-up, which has for its object the extinction, fall, breaking up and stopping of all conditioned processes, all the forms of becoming, all the forms of life, all the places of rebirth, all the stations of conscious life, all the abodes of sentient beings appear to him as one great source of danger, just as lions, and so on, appear to be a great source of danger to a timid man who wishes to live happily. . . . Even so, one who sees that the conditioned processes of the past have stopped, those of the present are stopping, and those that will arise in the future will also stop,—to him on that stage (of insight) there arises the cognition of the presence of danger.

Here is a simile to illustrate this : A woman had three sons who had offended the king. The king ordered them to be beheaded. She went with her sons to the place of the execution. When the head of the eldest son had been cut off, they proceeded to cut off that of the next-oldest. When she saw that the head of the eldest son had been cut off, and that they were in the process of beheading the next oldest one, she gave up all attachment to the youngest son, and thought that the same would happen to him as to them. (Just so is the attitude of the disciple to all conditioned processes.)

But when practising the cognition of the presence of danger one does not really become afraid. For one only recognizes the fact that the conditioned processes of the past have stopped, and that those of the future will also stop. When somebody sees near the city gate three pits full of live coals, he does not fear for himself, but only recognizes that all those who fall into them will experience not a little pain.

*4. The cognition of tribulation* (or peril (*ādīnava*))

He then understands that really there is no protection, no shelter, no way out, and no refuge in all the forms of becoming, all the forms of life, places of rebirth, stations of conscious life or all the abodes of sentient beings. Not a single one among all the conditioned processes in these forms of becoming, etc., is to him an object of aspiration, or can be misconstrued as a basis of his desire for security. The three forms of becoming appear to him like fiery pits filled with glowing coals; the four primary elements like poisonous snakes full of terrible poison; the five skandhas like murderers with their swords raised; the six inner sense-fields like an empty (deserted) village; the six outer sense-fields like robbers who devastate a village; the seven stations of conscious life and the nine abodes of sentient beings as though burning, ablaze and aflame with the eleven fires; and all conditioned things as a boil, a sickness, a dart, a misfortune, as oppressive, tasteless, insipid, just one large heap of peril.

And how? They appear to him as appears to a timid man who wishes to live happily a dense forest which is delightfully situated but haunted by wild beasts. Or like a cave inhabited by a panther, or like water filled with crocodiles and water sprites; like foes with their swords raised, like poisoned food, or a road invested by robbers, a burning house, or a battlefield occupied by armies ready to fight. For just as that man on account of the dense forest which is haunted by wild beasts, or in the other situations, becomes frightened, agitated and terrified, and sees only peril on all sides; just so this practitioner, when all conditioned things appear to him in the reviewing of breaking-up as dangerous, sees everywhere only what is tasteless, and insipid, peril on all sides.

'The genesis (of conditioned things), their proceeding,
their sign he views as ill;

And so their accumulation and reconception : this is the cognition of tribulation.
Their non-genesis, their non-proceeding, the absence of a sign of them he views as ease,
And so the absence of accumulation and of reconception : this is the cognition of the Path of Peace.'

That 'non-genesis is the cognition of the Path of Peace' has been said to show the cognition which is the opposite of the cognition of tribulation. Or it has been said so as to generate comfort in the hearts of those who have become anxious from having seen the peril (of all conditioned existence) as a result of the (insight into the) presence of danger, (by showing that) there is something which is not dangerous, which gives security, which is not perilous. Or it has been said to show the advantages of the cognition of tribulation which has been accomplished by the insight into the presence of danger, because, when genesis, etc., stand out to him clearly as dangerous, his mind is inclined to their opposites.

### 5. *The reviewing cognition of disgust*

When he thus sees all conditioned things as perilous, he turns away from everything that belongs to the conditioned things which are wont to break up and which are found in all forms of becoming, all forms of life, all the places of rebirth, stations of conscious life and abodes of sentient beings. He is dissatisfied with it, finds no pleasure in it. Just as the golden royal swan who finds his pleasure (in a fair pool) at the foot of Mount Splendid Spur (in the Himalayas) does not find any pleasure in the insalubrious mud puddle at the gate of a village of outcasts, but only in the seven great lakes; just so this Yogin, who is like a royal swan, takes no pleasure in all that belongs to the conditioned things which are wont to break up and of which he has well seen the peril; but he delights in the seven Reviewings, since he finds pleasure and delight in meditational development. And as a lion, the king of beasts, takes no pleasure in the golden cage into which it has been shut, but delights in the mountains of the Himalayas which extend over 3,000 miles; just so this Yogin, a true lion, finds no pleasure in the threefold becoming, pleasant though it may be, but he delights in the three Reviewings (of impermanence, ill, not-self). Or as a King Elephant, quite white, seven times supported, endowed with magical power and able to traverse the sky, with six tusks, takes no pleasure in the middle of a town, but delights in the deep lake of Chaddanta in the Himalayas; just so this Yogin, who is like a noble elephant, takes no pleasure in anything that belongs to conditioned things, but takes delight only in the Path of Peace, of which he has seen that 'non-genesis is Safety,' etc., and his mind is inclined to that, slopes towards that, is directed towards that.

*6. The cognition of the desire for release*

When the son of a good family by means of this cognition of disgust turns away from conditioned things, is dissatisfied with them, finds no more pleasure in them, then his heart does not cling, adhere or bind itself to even a single one among the conditioned processes which are wont to break up in all the forms of becoming, forms of life, places of rebirth, stations of conscious life, and abodes of sentient beings. But he wants to be released from all that belongs to conditioned things, wants to escape from it.

Wherewith could his attitude be compared? As a fish who has got himself into a net, a frog in a snake's mouth, a cock from the forest locked up in a cage, a deer in the power of a strong snare, a snake in the hands of a snake-charmer, an elephant sunk into a deep bog, a Naga-king in the mouth of the Garuda bird, the moon when it has entered into Rahu's mouth, or like a man surrounded by enemies,—just as all these want to be released from this or that danger, want to escape from it, just so the heart of that Yogin desires release and escape from all that belongs to conditioned things. The cognition of the desire for release then arises in him who is free from a desire to settle down in any of the conditioned things, and who wants to be released from all that belongs to them.

*7. The reviewing cognition of sizing-up*

In order to win this release he then again examines just those conditioned things by attributing to them the three marks by means of the reviewing cognition of sizing-up. Here this is a simile : A man who wanted to catch fish took an eel-basket and sank it into the water. After a time he put his hand into the opening of the eel-basket, seized under the water a snake by the neck and was glad to have caught a fish. He thought, 'great is the fish I have got here,' lifted it out of the water, looked at it, and recognized it as a snake by seeing the three svastikas on it. (3) He was frightened, (4) saw the danger he was in, (5) became disgusted with his catch, (6) and wanted to get rid of it. (7) So as to effect the means of getting rid of it, he then unwinds the snake from his arm, beginning with the tip of its tail, and then twice or three times swings it with his raised hand in a circle over his head. When he has thus weakened the snake, he flings it away with the words, 'Off with you, wretched snake !' He then quickly runs back to the shore, and there he looks back on the way he had come and thinks to himself, 'from the mouth of a great snake I have just now got away.'

Here, when the man was contented at having seized by the neck a snake he mistook for a fish, he is like the Yogin, when, in the beginning, he was contented at having got hold of his personality. As the man, after he had pulled out the head of the snake from the opening of the eel-basket, sees the three svastikas on it, so the Yogin sees the three marks in conditioned events, after he has made an analysis of what appeared as one lump. (The correspondence of the stages (3) to (6) is obvious.) (7) The effecting of the means for getting rid of the snake corresponds to the attribution of the three marks to conditioned events by means of the reviewing cognition of sizing-up. Just as that man, by whirling the snake about, weakens it, prevents it from biting him, and gets altogether rid of it, so also this practitioner, by whirling the conditioned events about as a result of attributing the three marks to them, weakens them, prevents them from again appearing in the modes of permanence, ease and attractiveness, and selfhood, and is altogether released of them. Therefore it has been said : He examines them in this way in order to achieve the means of release. And the throwing away of the snake corresponds to the cognition by which one becomes one of the saints ; his standing about, after he has got rid of it, when he looks back on the way he has come, corresponds to the cognition of the Path ; and his abiding in a place which is free from danger is the cognition of the Fruit.

### 8. *The cognition of evenmindedness as regards conditioned things*

When he has grasped conditioned things in such a way that he has seen them as empty (see IV 5), and attributed the three marks to them, he gives up both fear and delight, and becomes detached from conditioned things, and indifferent to them. He does not grasp them as 'I' or 'mine,' just as a man who has sent away his wife. Suppose a man has a wife, desirable, lovable and pleasing ; he cannot exist without her even for a moment, and he cherishes her exceedingly. When he sees her standing or sitting with another man, talking with him or laughing with him, he is offended and displeased, and experiences violent grief. At a later time he would see the faults of that woman, and wanting to be rid of her, would send her away, and he holds her no longer as his own. Henceforth when he sees her doing anything whatsoever with anyone whatsoever, he will not be offended, he will not feel any grief, and in all circumstances he remains detached and indifferent. Just so also this (Yogin) who wants to be released from all conditioned things, and who grasps conditioned things with the reviewing of sizing-up, who sees nothing in them that could be seized upon as I or mine, gives up both fear and delight, and becomes detached from all conditioned things, indifferent to them.

When he sees and cognizes things in such a way, his heart withdraws from the three forms of becoming, the four forms of life, the five places of rebirth, the seven stations of conscious life, the nine abodes of sentient beings; it becomes averse to them, turns away from them, does not reach out for them. But either evenmindedness or aversion is established.

And if this cognition of evenmindedness as to conditioned things sees the Path of Peace, Nirvana, as peaceful calm, it throws aside the whole proceeding of conditioned processes, and leaps forward into Nirvana. Otherwise it proceeds again and again with conditioned processes for its object.

Insight has now reached the summit, and it leads to emergence. . . . Because insight leads to the Path, therefore it leads to emergence. It joins up with the Path, that is the meaning.

First the *twofold* emptiness should be grasped, *i.e.*, that 'this is 1. empty of self, or 2. of anything belonging to a self' (M ii 263). In this way the disciple sees neither for himself nor for others anywhere anything which meets the requirements of selfhood.

Next he grasps the *fourfold* emptiness, which has been stated as: '1. I am not anywhere, 2. or anything to anybody, and 3. it is not mine anywhere, 4. nor is mine anything in any way' (M ii 263–4). How? 54. (1) For 'not I anywhere' means that he does not see his self in anything. (2) 'Or anything to anybody' means that he does not see that this self of his could be described as something to anybody in any respect, in other words, he does not see how it can be described on the occasion of thinking of a brother as a brother, of a friend as a friend, or of a belonging as a belonging (3) 'And not mine anywhere'; if one first leaves out the word 'mine,' the meaning is that he does not see the self of another anywhere in anything. (4) When one now brings in the word 'mine,' *i.e.*, 'nor is mine anything in any way,' that means that he does not see that the self of another belongs to him in any way whatsoever. Himself a brother considered as a brother, a friend considered as a friend, his belongings considered as belongings,—thus in any relationship whatsoever he does not see that the self of another can be ascribed to any state whatsoever,—that is the meaning. Thus because 1. he sees his own self nowhere, 2. does not see how it can be ascribed as belonging to another person in any way whatsoever, 3. does not see the self of another, 4. or that it can be ascribed to him in any way whatsoever, —therefore he has grasped the fourfold emptiness.

He then grasps emptiness *in six ways*. How? 'The eye is empty of 1. self, or 2. of anything belonging to self, or

3. of permanence, 4. of stability, 5. of everlastingness, 6. of non-liability to reversal . . . mind is empty . . . Sight-objects are empty . . . mind-objects are empty. . . . Eye-consciousness . . . mind-consciousness. . . . Eye-contact is empty . . .' (Nd ii 187), and thus the method should be taken as far as decay and death.

He then grasps emptiness *in eight ways,* namely : 'Form is unsubstantial, without substance, deprived of substance as regards 1. the substance of permanence, or 2. the substance of stability, 3. of ease, 4. of selfhood, or as regards 5. permanence, or 6. stability, or 7. everlastingness, or 8. non-liability to reversal. Feeling . . . consciousness, eye . . . decay and death are unsubstantial . . . reversal. Just as the hollow stalk of a reed is unsubstantial, without substance, deprived of substance, as a castor oil plant, as a fig tree, as a Setacaccha tree, as a Butea frondosa tree, as a mass of foam, as a water bubble, as a mirage, as a banana trunk, as a magic show is unsubstantial, without substance, deprived of substance, even so form . . . decay and death are unsubstantial . . . reversal' (Nd ii 184–5).

He then grasps emptiness *in ten ways.* How? 'He views form as 1. hollow, 2. vain, 3. empty, 4. not-self, 5. under no master, 6. something which cannot do as it wishes, 7. uncontrollable, 8. powerless, 9. alien, 10. apart. He views feeling . . . consciousness as hollow . . . apart' (Nd ii 279).

He then grasps emptiness *in twelve ways,* namely: 'Form is not 1. a being, not 2. a living soul, not 3. a man, not 4. a youth, not 5. a woman, not 6. a person, not 7. the self, not 8. anything belonging to self, not 9. I, not 10. mine, not 11. another's not 12. anybody's. Feeling . . . consciousness is not . . . anybody's' (Nd ii 186).

He then, through the scrutinising comprehension, grasps emptiness in *forty-two ways.* He views 'form as 1. impermanent, suffering, disease, boil, barb, misery, affliction, alien, crumbling, 10. calamity, troublesome, terrible, misfortune, shaky, brittle, unstable, no protection, no shelter, no refuge, 20. (no safe refuge), hollow, vain, empty, not-self, (unsatisfactory), tribulation, liable to reversal, unsubstantial, root of misery, 30. murderous, one's undoing, with outflows, conditioned, Mara's bait, liable to birth, liable to decay, liable to illness, liable to death, liable to sorrow, lamentation, pain, sadness and despair, 40. (as to origination, as to passing away, as to the escape from it). He views feeling ... consciousness as impermanent ... escape from it' (cf. Pts ii 238).

He contemplates each skandha 1. as *impermanent*, because it has no perpetuity, but a beginning and end; 2. as *suffering*, because it is molested by rise and fall, and is a basis of suffering; 3. as *a disease*, because (its health) depends on conditions, and it is a source of disease; 4. as *a boil*, because it is impaled on the stake of suffering, exudes the impurities of the defilements, and, as it originates, decays and breaks up, it swells up, ripens and bursts; 5. as *a barb*, because it is productive of injury, pierces the inside, and is hard to extract; 6. as *a misery*, because it is blameworthy, brings deterioration, and is a basis for misery; 7. as an *affliction*, because it is productive of states which are not to one's liking, and is a proximate cause of affliction; 8. as *alien*, because it is unruly and cannot be managed; 9. as *crumbling*, because it crumbles away through illness, decay and death;

10. as a *calamity*, because it brings many misfortunes; 11. as *troublesome*, because it brings an abundance of yet unknown disadvantages, and is a basis for all troubles; 12. as *terrible*, because in it all terrors are stored up, and it is opposed to the highest comfort known as the appeasing of suffering; 13. as a *misfortune*, because it is bound up with many disadvantages, and faults are attached to it; and, because like a misfortune, it does not deserve that one should tolerate it gladly; 14. as *shaky*, because it is

shaken by illness, decay and death, and by (the eight) worldly conditions, such as gain, loss, etc.; 15. as *brittle*, because it has the property to disintegrate both under attacks from outside, and through its own inherent nature; 16. as *unstable*, because it may fall down at any stage, and has no solidity; 17. as *no protection*, because it cannot give any protection, and no security can be obtained from it; 18. as *no shelter*, because it does not deserve that one should stick to it, and because it does not provide a shelter for those who do stick to it; 19. as *no refuge*, because it does not remove the dangers of those who rely on it;

20. as *hollow*, because it is destitute of such stability, attractiveness, ease and selfhood as are imagined; 21. as *vain*, either because it is destitute of these, or because it is trifling; for in the world a trifling thing is called 'vain'; 22. as *empty*, because it is devoid of an owner, one who resides in it, a doer, a feeler, a manager; 23, as *not-self*, because it has itself not owner, etc.; 24. as *tribulation*, on account of the sufferings of the process of the round of births, and the tribulation from (that) suffering. Or, 'tribulation' (*ādīnava*) means wretchedness (*ādīna*) spreads (*vā-ti*), goes on, proceeds: it is a term used to designate a particularly wretched human being; and since also the skandhas are wretched, like that human being, they therefore amount to a tribulation; 25. as *liable to reversal*, because it has the nature to be reversed through the two factors of decay and death; 26. as *unsubstantial*, because of its weakness, and because, like bark, it breaks easily; 27. as a *root of misery*, because it is a root-condition of misery; 28. as *murderous*, because, like a foe with a friendly face, it kills those who trust it; 29. as *one's undoing*, because it does not help one along, and renders one's undoing possible;

30. as *with outflows*, because it is a proximate cause of

the outflows; 31. as *conditioned,* because it is effected by a combination of causes and conditions; 32. as *Mara's bait,* because it is truly the bait of the Mara who brings death, and of the Mara who represents the defilements; 33.–36. as *liable to birth, decay, illness, and death,* because its nature brings birth, decay, illness and death with it; 37.–39. as *liable to sorrow, lamentation and despair,* because it is the root-cause of sorrow, lamentation and despair; 40. as *liable to the defilements,* because it is doomed to be the province of the defilements of craving, wrong views, and misconduct.

# NUMERICAL LISTS

2 *Extremes:* 1. eternity, 2. annihilation; or 1. indulgence in sense pleasure, 2. ascetic self-torment.

3 *Becomings:* 1. with sense-desire, 2. with form, 3. without form; or: 1. with perception, 2. without perception, 3. with neither perception nor non-perception.—pp. 144, 168

3 *kinds of Concentration:* 1. momentary, 2. access, 3 ecstasy.—p. 114

3 *Doors of action:* 1. body, 2. speech, 3. mind.—p. 131

3 *Fires* = 3 Roots of evil.—p. 143

3 *kinds of Knowledge:* 1. Memory of past lives, 2. heavenly eye, 3. extinction of the outflows.—p. 46

3 *Marks of all conditioned things:* 1. rise, 2. persistence, 3. fall.—p. 144.—or: 1. impermanence, 2. ill, 3. not-self.—p. 146

3 *Roots of evil:* 1. greed, 2. hate, 3. delusion.

3 *Treasures:* 1. Buddha, 2. Dharma, 3. Samgha.

3 *Worlds:* 1. world of sense-desire, 2. world of form, 3. formless world.

4 *Applications of Mindfulness:* Concerning 1. the body, 2. feelings, 3. thoughts, 4. dharmas.

4 *Effluvia:* 1. bile, 2. phlegm, 3. pus, 4. blood.

4 *Forms of life:* 1. from eggs, 2. from a womb, 3. from moisture, 4. apparitionally born.—pp. 108, 168

4 *Formless attainments:* 1. Endless space, 2. infinite consciousness, 3. nothing whatever, 4. neither perception nor non-perception.

4 *Fruits:* Fruits of the 4 Paths, i.e., fruit of a streamwinner, etc.

4 *kinds of Grasping:* Described pp. 155–6

4 *Jhanas:* First, second, third, fourth.

4 *Pairs of men:* Those established in the 4 Paths and the 4 Fruits.

4 *Paths:* 1. Streamwinner, 2. Once-returner, 3. Never-returner, 4. Arhat.

4 *Perverted Views:* They see 1. permanence in the impermanent, 2. ease in what is ill, 3. the self in what is without self, 4. attraction in what is repulsive.

4 *Postures:* 1. standing, 2. walking, 3. sitting, 4. lying down.

4 *(material) Primaries:* 1. earth, 2. water, 3, fire, 4. air.

4 *Stations of Brahma:* 1. friendliness, 2. compassion, 3. sympathetic joy, 4. evenmindedness.

4 *holy Truths:* 1. ill, 2. origination of ill, 3. stopping of ill, 4. path that leads to the stopping of ill.

4 *Unlimited* = 4 Stations of Brahma.

5 *Doors of the Dharma:* List on p. 15

5 *Hindrances:* 1. sense-desire, 2. ill will, 3. sloth and torpor, 4. excitedness and sense of guilt, 5. doubt (indecision).

5 *Jhana-limbs:* 1. applied thinking, 2. discursive thinking, 3. rapture, 4. joy, 5. one-pointedness of thought.—p. 115; but see p. 48

5 *Places of rebirth:* 1. beings in the hells, 2. animals, 3. pretas, 4. men, 5. devas.—pp. 108, 168

5 *kinds of Rapture:* Enumerated p. 114

5 *Sense-qualities:* 1. forms, 2. sounds, 3. smells, 4. tastes, 5. touchables.

5 *Skandhas:* 1. form, 2. feelings, 3. perceptions, 4. impulses, 5. consciousness.

5 *(cardinal) Virtues:* 1. faith, 2. vigour, 3. mindfulness, 4. concentration, 5. wisdom.

6 *Recollections:* Recollection of 1. the Buddha, 2. the Dharma, 3. the Samgha, 4. Morality, 5. Liberality, 6. Devas.—p. 108

6 *Sense-objects:* 1. forms, 2. sounds, 3. smells, 4. tastes, 5. touchables, 6. mind-objects.

6 *Sense-organs:* 1. eye, 2. ear, 3. nose, 4. tongue, 5. body, 6. mind.

7 *Buddhas:* 1. Vipassin, 2. Sikhin, 3. Vessabhū, 4. Kakusandha, 5. Kanakamuni, 6. Kassapa, 7. Sakyamuni.—p. 82

7 *Good Dharmas:* 1. faith, 2. vigour, 3. sense of shame, 4. dread of blame, 5. mindfulness, 6. concentration, 7. wisdom.—p. 46

7 *Limbs of Enlightenment:* 1. mindfulness, 2. investigation into dharma, 3. vigour, 4. joyous zest, 5. tranquillity, 6. concentration, 7. evenmindedness.

7*-fold Office:* 1. salutation, 2. worship, 3. confession of sins, 4. rejoicing, 5. entreaty, 6. raising the heart to enlightenment, 7. dedication of merit.—p. 135; see I 3

7 *Stations of Conscious Life:* 1. diverse in both body and mind (men, ghosts, etc.); 2. diverse in body, uniform in mind (Brahmabodied Devas); 3. uniform in body, diverse in mind (Radiant Devas); 4. uniform in both body and mind (Lustrous Devas); 5. those born in the station of endless space; 6. those born in the station of infinite consciousness; 7. those born in the station of nothing whatever.—pp. 108, 163, 168

8 *Great Hells:* 8 places of punishment for people who have committed various offences, e.g., Sañjiva for murderers, Kālasūtra for liars, and so on.—p. 121

8 *Kinds of Knowledge:* 1. Insight-cognition, 2. the ability to conjure up mind-made bodies, 3. wonderworking powers, 4. heavenly ear, 5. knowledge of the hearts of others, 6. memory of past lives, 7. heavenly eye, 8. knowledge of the extinction of the outflows.—p. 46

8*-fold Path:* 1. right views, 2. right intentions, 3. right speech, 4. right conduct, 5. right livelihood, 6. right effort, 7. right mindfulness, 8. right concentration.

8 *Worldly Conditions:* 1. gain, 2. loss, 3. respect, 4. contempt, 5. good luck, 6. bad luck, 7. praise, 8. blame.—p. 171

9 *Abodes of Sentient Beings:* 1. men, devas, beings in hell; 2. Brahmabodied Gods; 3. Abhasvara Gods; 4. Subhakinha Gods; 5. beings without perception; 6. those born in the station of endless space; 7. those born in the station of infinite consciousness; 8. those born in the station of nothing whatever; 9. those born in the station of neither perception nor non-perception.—pp. 108, 163, 168

9-*fold Supramundane Dharma:* 4 Paths, 4 Fruits, Nirvana.

10 *Devices (kasina):* List on p. 14

10 *Recollections:* List on p. 14

10 *Repulsive things:* List on p. 14

10 *Directions:* East, West, North, South; North-East, North-West, South-West, South-East; above, below.

11 *kinds of Form:* 1. past, 2. present, 3. future; 4. inward, 5. outward; 6. gross, 7. refined; 8. low, 9. exalted; 10. distant, 11, near.—pp. 146–7

12 *Links of Conditioned co-production:* 1. ignorance, 2. karma-formations, 3. consciousness, 4. name-and-form, 5. six sense-fields, 6. contact, 7. feeling, 8. craving, 9. grasping, 10. becoming, 11. birth, 12. decay and death.

12 *Sense-fields:* 6 Sense-organs + 6 sense-objects.

16 *Aspects of the four truths:* Enumerated in IV 1b.

16 *Ussada hells:* 16 places of punishment which differ according to the torture inflicted in them.—p. 121

18 *Elements:* 6 sense-organs + 6 sense-objects + 6 kinds of sense-consciousness.

30 *Perfections:* The 10 perfections (*pāramī*) are: 1. giving, 2. morality, 3. renunciation, 4. wisdom, 5. vigour, 6. patience, 7. truth(fulness), 8. sustaining power, 9. friendliness, 10. evenmindedness. In their more intense form they appear first as the 10 *upapāramī,* and then as the 10 *paramatthapāramī.* —p. 147

32 *Parts of the body:* Enumerated in II 5a.

32 *kinds of Torture:* Enumerated in M xiii, p. 87.—p. 140

40 *Subjects of meditation:* List on p. 14

# SOURCES

I, 1a.—VM vii 2, 5–6, 22–4, 26, 30–4, 36, 46–7, 49, 52–3, 65–7
I, 1b.—VM vii 68–9, 73–4, 76, 79, 80, 82, 84–5
I, 1c.—VM vii 89, 90, 92–3, 98
I, 2. —VM ix 25–35
I, 3. —Bcv. II 1–6, 24–6, 48–9; 27–9; iii 1–10, 22–3
II, 1a.—Ps X no. 58–98 (summary)
II, 1b.—VM viii 159, 160, 162, 190–3, 195–7, 202, 204–8, 210, 214–16, 220, 238
II, 2a.—Ps X no. 108, 114–15, 117
II, 2b.—Ps X no. 122–32
II, 3a.—VM i 42, 53–9, 100, 104–5, 108
II, 3b.—M XX and Ps XX (summary)
II, 3c.—Bc xi 23–9
II, 4. —VM viii 3–17, 25–41
II, 5a.—VM viii 48–50, 56–9, 62, 65–6, 81–8, 139, 140, 144
II, 5b.—VM xi 5, 6, 16, 19–22, 26
II, 5c.—VM vi 1, 85, 87–90
II, 6. —VM viii 245–8, 250–1
III, 1a.—Bcv. viii 1–16, 24, 26–9, 33–4, 38–9
III, 1b.—VM iv 94, 98–100, 106–8, 124–5, 141–4, 148
III, 2a.—VM ix 15–20, 22–5, 36–7, 60–4, 70–1, 73–6
III, 2b.—VM ix 1–8, 10–12, 14, 40–1, 43–4, 46–52
III, 2c.—VM ix 78–80
III, 2d.—VM ix 85–6
III, 2e.—VM ix 88–90
III, 3. —Sm no. 98, pp. 201–6
IV, 1a.—VM xvi, 34–45, 47, 58, 60
IV, 1b.—AK vii 13
IV, 2a.—VM xx 13–17
IV, 2b.—VM xx 47
IV, 3a.—DhS 597–616; VM xv 39; Śi. 225; LS p. 44
IV, 3b.—VM xv 15; Si. 225; VM xviii 31
IV, 3c.—VM xvii (summary)
IV, 4. —VM xx 93–9, 103–4; xxi 10, 11, 24, 27, 29, 30, 32, 35–7, 40, 43, 45–7, 49, 50, 93, 61–3, 65, 83
IV, 5. —VM xxi 53–9; xx 19



M

# ABBREVIATIONS

| | | |
|---|---|---|
| A | = | Anguttara Nikāya |
| AK | = | Abhidharmakośa |
| Bc | = | Buddhacarita |
| Bcv | = | Bodhicaryāvatāra |
| D | = | Dīgha Nikāya |
| Dh-A | = | Dhammapada Aṭṭhakathā |
| Dhp | = | Dhammapada |
| DhS | = | Dhammasangani |
| LS | = | Lankāvatāra Sūtra |
| M | = | Majjhima Nikāya |
| Nd | = | Niddesa |
| Ps | = | Papañcasūdanī |
| Pts | = | Paṭisambhidāmagga |
| PTS | = | Pali Text Society |
| S | = | Samyutta Nikāya |
| Śi | = | Śikshāsamuccaya |
| Sm | = | Sādhanamālā |
| Sn | = | Sutta Nipāta |
| T | = | Taishō Issaikyō |
| Th | = | Theragāthā |
| VM | = | Visuddhimagga |

# EDITIONS USED[1]


ÁŚVAGHOSA (*ca* 150 A.D.), BUDDHACARITA, ed. E. H. Johnston, Calcutta 1936
E: E. H. Johnston, 1936

BUDDHAGHOSA (*ca* 400 A.D.), VISUDDHIMAGGA, ed. H. C. Warren, HOS, 1950
G: Visuddhimagga, oder, Der Weg zur Reinheit. uebs. Nyanatiloka, Verlag Christiani, Konstanz 1952
E: The Path of Purity, trsl. Pe Maung Tin, I–III, PTS, 1923–31

BUDDHAGHOSA, PAPAÑCASŪDANĪ, MAJJHIMANIKĀYATTHAKATHĀ, ed. J. H. Woods and D. Kosambi, I, 1922, II, 1928.
E: I, 10: trsl. Bhikkhu Soma, The way of mindfulness, 2nd ed., Colombo 1949

DHAMMASANGANI (*ca* 100 B.C.), ed. PTS 1885
E: C. A. F. Rhys Davids, A Buddhist Manual of Psychological Ethics, 1900

LANKĀVATĀRA SŪTRA (*ca* 350 A.D.), ed. B. Nanjio, Kyoto 1923
E: trsl. D. T. Suzuki, L 1932

MAJJHIMA NIKĀYA, ed. PTS 1887–1907
E: trsl. Lord Chalmers, Further Dialogues of the Buddha, 1926–27

SĀDHANAMĀLĀ, ed. B. Bhattacharya, I, Baroda, 1925
no. 98: Kiṃcit-vistara-Tārā-sādhanā, by Anupama Rakshita.
E: B. Bhattacharya, The Indian Buddhist Iconography, 1924, pp. 169–75
A. K. Coomaraswamy, Figures of speech or figures of thought, 1946, pp. 146–51

ŚĀNTIDEVA (*ca* 750), BODHICARYĀVATĀRA, ed. together with Prajñākaramati's commentary, by L. de la Vallée-Poussin, Calcutta 1901–14
E: partly trsl. as *The Path of Light,* by L. Barnett, L 1909

ŚĀNTIDEVA, ŚIKSHĀSAMUCCAYA, ed. C. Bendall, St. Petersbourg 1897–1902
E: C. Bendall and W. H. D. Rouse, L 1922

VASUBANDHU (*ca* 400), ABHIDHARMAKOŚA, traduit et annoté par L. de la Vallée-Poussin, chapters VII to IX, 1925


[1]For the convenience of readers I have added the main translations, so that they can easily find the context of my selections.

# GLOSSARY OF TECHNICAL TERMS

Abhidharma: 'Further Dharma,' or 'Higher Dharma.' The books on Abhidharma deal with the contemplation of events as carried out by wisdom.

Access: The initial stage of trance.

Adaptation: The stage of insight which follows immediately on the 'cognition of evenmindedness' described on pp. 167–8.

Adoption: The stage of spiritual development which immediately precedes that of a Streamwinner.

Aeon: A very long period of time, a 'world-age.'

Amida: A Buddha who rules over a world-system in the West. The 'Amida school,' very strong in China and Japan, is devoted to his cult.

Arahat, or Arhat: The perfect saint.

Ardhaparyanka posture: The position is like the one familiar from the images of seated Buddhas, but the right leg is more relaxed.

Ariyan: A saint, a 'noble' or 'holy' man.

Being = a living being.

Bhaktic: A form of Buddhism based on the loving personal devotion to adored deities conceived in human form.

Bodhi: sanskrit for enlightenment.

Bodhi-being = Bodhi-sattva.

Bodhi-tree: The tree under which the Buddha won enlightenment.

Bodhisattva: A person on his way to enlightenment. A Buddha before he has won enlightenment.

Brahmā: A very high deity.

Ch'an school: A Chinese school founded *ca* 500 A.D., and better known by the Japanese name of Zen.

Concentration: Two kinds described pp. 19–21.

Conditioned co-production: A general term for the 12 'links' which connect suffering with ignorance.

Deva: A 'god,' 'deity' or 'angel.' Literally: 'A Shining One.' There are many thousands and millions of Devas.

Devices: Arrangements for inducing trance. See p. 21.

Dharma: 1. The one ultimate reality; 2. the doctrine of the Buddha. 3. A dharma, or a 'dharmic constituent of the universe' is a thing as it appears when viewed by wisdom.

Dharma-body: The Buddha conceived as the Absolute.

Dhyāna: The sanskrit form of Jhāna.

Dīpankara: A Buddha, the 24th predecessor of the historical Buddha.

Ecstasy: Full transic concentration.

Extinction of the Outflows: A synonym of Arhatship.

Formless: Those levels of the universe in which matter is absent.—The higher stages of trance.

Garuda: A mythical bird.

Guru: A spiritual teacher.

Hathayoga: A branch of Yoga which aims at establishing conscious control over the automatic processes of the body.

Hindrances: Those mental states which prevent trance.

Jina: An epithet of the Buddha, meaning 'Conqueror.'

Jhānas: The successive stages of transic concentration.

Kammatthana: A subject of meditation.

Karma: Those deeds which lead to either reward or punishment.

Mara: The personification of evil.

Mental Image: An object as it appears on the higher levels of trance.

Mindfulness: Described, p. 28 *sq*.

Moral Rules, or, Moral Precepts: The five commandments, which forbid the taking of life, etc.

Naked Ascetics: Non-Buddhist ascetics, Jains and others, who practice self-torture.

Naga-king: A king of the Serpents.

Never-returner: A saint who, after death, does not return again to this world, but wins Nirvana elsewhere.

Nikāya: The principal divisions of the Canon of the Theravadins are called 'nikāyas,' literally 'collections.'

Observance-day: The 1st, 8th, 15th and 23rd day of the lunar month. On these days Buddhist laymen pledge themselves to observe eight special rules of conduct.

Old Wisdom School: The Buddhism of Theravadins and Sarvastivadins.

Period = aeon.

Pranayama exercises: Yogic breathing exercises.

Pratyekabuddha: Someone who, like a Buddha, is fully enlightened, but who, unlike a Buddha, is either unable or unwilling to teach.

Rahu: A planet, normally invisible, which is held to account for eclipses of the sun or moon.

Śakra: A name for Indra, one of the Devas.

Samādhi: sanskrit for 'transic concentration.'

Samgha: The order of monks.—The more technical meaning is explained at p. 28.

Samsara: This conditioned world in which we wander about from life to life.

Sarvastivadins: A Buddhist school formerly very strong in the North-West of India.

Satori: A Japanese Zen term for the sudden awakening to the meaning of life.

Skandhas: The five constituents of the personality. See pp. 33–4.

Streamwinner: The lowest kind of saint, who has just made contact with the Unconditioned.

Sugata: An epithet of the Buddha, 'Well-gone' or 'Well-farer.'

Supramundane: Thoughts are supramundane to the extent that they are governed by the Absolute.

Sutra: A text which claims to have been taught by the Buddha himself.

Sutta: The Pali form of 'Sutra.'

Tantra: A form of Buddhism in which magical beliefs and rituals hold a prominent place.

Tathagata: A title of the Buddha.

Terrace of enlightenment: The place on which the Buddha won enlightenment.

Thera: An old and revered monk.

Theravādin: A Buddhist school, now dominant in Ceylon, who claim to 'teach' (-vādin) what the Theras of old had taught.

Tripitaka: The Buddhist Scriptures, divided into three parts, or 'baskets': Vinaya, Sutra, Abhidharma.

Vinaya: The rules of monastic discipline. The first section of the Tripitaka.

Wisdom: Described p. 33 *sq*.